DA CAPO PRESS SERIES IN
ARCHITECTURE AND DECORATIVE ART

General Editor: Adolf K. Placzek
Avery Librarian, Columbia University

Volume 25

AUTOBIOGRAPHY OF
JAMES GALLIER
ARCHITECT

New Orleans from St. Patrick's Church, 1852

AUTOBIOGRAPHY OF
JAMES GALLIER
ARCHITECT

With a New Introduction by Samuel Wilson, Jr.
and a Supplement of Illustrations

DA CAPO PRESS · NEW YORK · 1973

Library of Congress Cataloging in Publication Data

Gallier, James.
    Autobiography of James Gallier, architect.

(Da Capo Press series in architecture and decorative
art, v. 25)
    Reprint of the 1864 ed.
    1. Gallier, James.
NA737.G34A2   1973   720'.92'4   69-13715
ISBN 0-306-71247-4

This Da Capo Press edition of the
Autobiography of James Gallier, Architect,
is an unabridged republication of the first
edition published in Paris in 1864.

INTRODUCTION

The name of James Gallier (1798–1866), though little known beyond the limits of the city where most of his work was done, has been regarded in New Orleans for over a century as synonymous with the classic architecture for which that city is justly renowned. Gallier's brief career of scarcely fifteen years of active practice in New Orleans was brought to an untimely end about the middle of the century by failing eyesight; but his gifted son, James Gallier, Jr., successfully carried on his work as a distinguished architect-builder until after the Civil War. Few, perhaps, even among those to whom the Gallier name is familiar, are aware that it belongs to two architects, father and son, each designing in the style of his own generation and each producing works of distinction, some of which still survive as treasured landmarks, but many of which have disappeared through fire or the wrecker's hammer, victims of the hand of time and relentless progress.

After his retirement from active practice as an architect, Gallier spent the remaining years of his life mostly in foreign travel, but he also devoted some of his leisure time to the writing of an autobiography, which he published in Paris in 1864. The edition was probably quite limited, and the few extant copies are to be found only in rare book repositories. Its republication at this time of accelerated urban growth, unequaled since the time Gallier first arrived in America in 1832, will be of interest not only to the architectural historian, but also to all who have an interest in social progress and the development of the arts in America.

Gallier must have had a genuine awareness of the interesting times in which he lived and the importance of his contribution to the beautification of his adopted city. New Orleans in turn has shown its appreciation in many ways, including naming a street for him and bestowing his name upon one of his last great works, the old City Hall on Lafayette Square, which was designated Gallier Hall after the new City Hall was erected in 1956.

When Gallier's "Municipality Hall" was completed in 1850, it was but one of the many works of his genius then adorning the city. Looking from the top of the lofty Gothic tower of St. Patrick's Church with the artist B.F. Smith, Jr., whose view of the city from that vantage point was published in 1852 (see frontispiece), numerous buildings designed by Gallier alone, or in partnership with Charles Bingley Dakin, are conspicuously evident. St. Patrick's itself, though begun in 1837 by Dakin and his brother, James H. Dakin, was completed by Gallier, who took over the project in 1839. Its 185-foot tower, for years the tallest structure in New Orleans, overshadows the nearby Presbyterian Church facing Lafayette Square, begun in November, 1834, and destroyed by fire in 1854. This fine church, with its Wren-like spire, has not been identified conclusively as the work of Gallier and Dakin; but its classic style, with a Greek Doric recessed porch, lends plausibility to the attribution. There is some evidence that it may have been designed by George Clarkson, who was killed in an encounter with A. T. Wood, the architect selected over Gallier for the New Orleans Custom House.

Gallier's City Hall appears beyond the church, and farther down St. Charles Street is his Commercial Exchange (later the Masonic Temple) built in 1845. Next to it looms the huge mass of the St. Charles Hotel, designed by Gallier and Dakin in 1835, a building whose dome was the admiration of travelers arriving by the river.

In the distance on Canal Street, at the left of the hotel, stands the Gothic spire of Christ Church, built by Gallier in 1847 from plans drawn by the architect-diarist Thomas K. Wharton; and at the right, at Canal and Bourbon, is the fine Ionic portico of the previous home of Christ Church, built in 1835 by Daniel H. Twogood from the designs of Gallier and Dakin.

In the background, on Royal just below Canal, rises the low dome of the Merchants' Exchange, crowning one of the first great monumental interior spaces ever seen in New Orleans. Farther away are seen two of the principal works of Gallier's chief rival, French architect J.N.B. De Pouilly, whose St. Louis Hotel of 1835 and St. Louis Cathedral, rebuilt in 1850, were the Creole counterparts to the St. Charles Hotel and St. Patrick's which represented the challenge of the growing American segment of the population.

James Gallier was an Irishman, a native of Ravensdale, where he was born in 1798. Mostly self-educated, he learned the building trades from his father, and while working in Dublin and in Liverpool, he must have been impressed early by the magnificence of the new classic architecture of those cities. After working for some years in England, where his son, James, Jr., was born in 1827, he decided to seek new opportunity in America.

Upon his arrival in New York in 1832, Gallier began his career with James Harrison Dakin, a former partner in the firm of Ithiel Town and Alexander Jackson Davis, then among the foremost American exponents of the architecture of the Greek Revival. After a brief association with Minard Lafever, whose builders' handbooks did so much to spread the Greek Revival throughout the country, Gallier decided in 1834 to come to New Orleans with C.B. Dakin. The two quickly became the favored architects of the American community, then led largely by wealthy Irish merchants, and they found opportunity and success beyond their fondest expectations. In their first year in the booming port and commercial center of the South, they received commissions for an incredible number of their most important buildings. Subsequently, with the arrival of Dakin's brother in New Orleans, Gallier and the Dakins decided to go their separate ways, each continuing to produce splendid Gothic and Greek Revival structures. Gallier's crowning work was his New Orleans City Hall; and J.H. Dakin's was his Gothic State Capitol at Baton Rouge, on which he was engaged at the time of his death in 1852. (C.B. Dakin had died in 1839.)

Gallier's life ended tragically in 1866 when, returning to New Orleans with his wife on the steamer *Evening Star,* the ship was lost in a hurricane off Cape Hatteras with all on board. (This was the same place where he and his son had nearly met with a marine disaster in 1849.) His son erected an impressive marble cenotaph in St. Louis Cemetery No. 3 to the memory of his distinguished father and stepmother. It soon after became his own tomb, for James Gallier, Jr., noted principally for his design of the old French Opera House in 1859, met an untimely death in 1868, leaving several daughters in whose families the Gallier name is still preserved.

So well known did James Gallier become as perhaps the chief architect-builder of mid-nineteenth century New Orleans that most Greek Revival buildings of the period were popularly attributed to him. His identified works, however, and the fine collection of his drawings in the Sylvester Labrot Collection at Tulane University, as well as his fascinating autobiography, are more than enough to secure for him an important place in the architectural and social history of the United States.

Much of the confusion connected with Gallier's life and works can be attributed to the small amount of scholarly research that has been published regarding his career. As Talbot Hamlin points out in his *Greek Revival Architecture in America,* however, Gallier's "privately printed *Autobiography* gives priceless details on the conditions of architectural practice in America as well as on the history of the development of New Orleans. . . ." Perhaps its republication at this time will stimulate renewed interest in his work and will produce a definitive biography that will answer many of the questions left unresolved or even unmentioned in his own writings.

The only other published work concerning Gallier is a catalogue issued by the Louisiana Landmarks Society in 1950 on the occasion of an exhibition of photographs, drawings, and general memorabilia presented in commemoration of the centennial of the New Orleans City Hall. Gallier himself, however, published *The American Builder's General Price Book and Estimator* in 1833 before leaving New York for New Orleans. In it, according to Marion Dean Ross of the University of Oregon, who wrote the introduction to the 1950 catalogue, Gallier expressed a genuine professional attitude toward architecture, writing that "I hold it to be a duty incumbent on every one connected with the Art to attempt an addition to the general stock of knowledge; and be that addition ever so little, it will tend to advance the profession, and ultimately prove beneficial to the public."

Gallier lost money on his *Price Book;* but in pursuit of his interest in advancing the profession and benefiting the public, he prepared a series of lectures on architecture and architectural history, the manuscripts of which are now in the Labrot Collection at Tulane. Gallier gave these lectures a few times in public; and to advertise his venture into the field of architectural education, he published and distributed a small handbill:

Popular Lectures
on
Architecture
by
J. Gallier, Architect

The first of a Course of Seven Lectures on Architecture, will be given in the Large Room of the Classical Hall, Washington Street, Brooklyn, on Tuesday Evening, the 25 of February, to commence at half-past seven o'clock, and to be continued on the evenings of every Friday and Tuesday, until the Course is completed.

Then followed a synopsis of each lecture, the last one including remarks on "Architecture in America; its future prospects, and the means required to bring it to perfection." At the foot of the handbill he announced: "Admission for the Course One Dollar, and for a Single Lecture, 25 cents."

Other research material that could throw additional light on Gallier's life and works can be found in numerous records on file in the Civil Courts Building in New Orleans. There, in the Notarial Archives, at least fifty building contracts were recorded by the Gallier firm. The Archives also contain partnership agreements, including one passed before the notary H.B. Cenas on May 4, 1836, between James Gallier and Michael Collins — articles of copartnership "in the art or trade of building, and all things thereunto belonging: — and also in the business, interest and property of a planing machine ... under the style and firm of Gallier & Collins." This co-partnership was dissolved by another notarial act on April 14, 1838. In addition, there is the power of attorney Gallier granted to John Turpin (later his son's partner), probably at the time when his eyesight began to fail, and the records of various court cases in which both Gallier and Dakin figured, sometimes as litigants and sometimes as witnesses. The available documentary information and the remaining buildings make it amply clear why Gallier has always been considered one of New Orleans' best known and respected architects.

So greatly has interest in historic preservation increased —particularly in the works of the Galliers—in recent years that in 1969 a New Orleans Foundation purchased the fine Vieux Carre residence at 1132 Royal Street built by James Gallier, Jr. for himself in 1857 and where his father undoubtedly visited in his later years. The house has been carefully restored and furnished as it is believed to have been during Gallier's lifetime and opened as a historic house museum in 1971. The adjacent buildings have also been added to the Gallier House Complex which has become a center for the study of the works of both Galliers and of the nineteenth century cultural life of New Orleans.

New Orleans   Samuel Wilson, Jr.
March, 1973

AUTOBIOGRAPHY

OF

JAMES GALLIER

AUTOBIOGRAPHY

OF

JAMES GALLIER

ARCHITECT

—⁂—

PARIS

PRINTED BY E. BRIERE,

257, Rue Saint-Honoré, 257.

—

1864

AUTOBIOGRAPHY

OF

JAMES GALLIER

ARCHITECT,

A traditional record, long in our family, asserts that at a remote period our progenitors with others fled from Gaul to escape the tyranny of the Romans; that they proceeded westward, first into Wales, and thence into Ireland, where the habits and religion of the people so closely resembling their own, they settled upon tracts of land that had been liberally yielded to them by the hospitable Irish; that there are places in the county of Limerick called *Gall Baile*, or Gaul's town, and *Baile na Francoigh*, or Frank's town, which may probably indicate the localities where the refugees established themselves; that among those refugees was one who afterwards became a famous general, *Gealta Gooth* (the Galacus of Tacitus), and that he commanded the Irish forces sent to the assistance of the Picts and Scots, when they so successfully repulsed on the Grampian

Hills the overwhelming legions of Rome, who were never afterwards able to penetrate farther into North Britain.

Our name, *Gallier*, may still be found in those parts of France that stretch along the Pyrénées, and in Britanny. When certain portions of Ireland were conquered, and taken possession of by the English, this name, Gallier, took in the English language, as then spoken in Ireland, the more guttural sound of Gallagher, which it has retained to the present time; while in the Irish language, it was always called *Galthan*, or *Mac Galthan* (literally a descendant, or son of the Gaul), and in the vernacular Irish it is so called to the present day (1).

(1) Parmi les nations descendues des Gaulois qui ont conservé le nom de ces peuples avec une légère altération, nous comptons les *Wallois* ou *Gallois* d'Angleterre ; les *Wallons* ou *Gallo-Belges*, les *Wallaches* de la Hongrie ; les *Galliriens* ou *Gallowaidiens* d'Irlande ; Gallowaidiens d'Ecosse, nommés dans les auteurs latins Gael-Walli, et *Galoridii ;* les *Galiciens* de Pologne, les Galiciens d'Espagne, en latin Gallaici ; les Galates d'Asie ; les Wesphaliens d'Allemagne, etc.

(*Recherches sur les origines celtiques du Bugey considéré comme berceau du Delta celtique*, par Pierre BACON-TACON. Paris, an VI).

Les désinences en IER sont très-fréquentes dans la nomenclature celtique, et souvent y présentent un sens équivoque, qui pourtant, à l'analyse, est susceptible d'une solution. Il faut donc savoir que cette désinence appartient, selon les différents cas, tantôt à la nomenclature sacrée, tantôt à la nomenclature vulgaire ou profane. Dans le premier cas, *ier* signifie *hiéreus* ou *sacerdos*, et indique une dénomination sacerdotale ; témoin Ségu ier, qui signifie *Victoriæ pontifex ;* dans le second, *ier* indique un office civil ou militaire ou un simple métier, et répond aux désinences en *arius* de la nomenclature latine, comme *centenier* (centenarius), huissier (ostiarius) ; c'est donc le sens de la désinence dans tous les noms terminés en IER.

(*Révolutions des peuples de l'Asie moyenne, influence de leurs migrations sur l'état social de l'Europe*, par A. JARDOT, capitaine du corps royal d'état-major. Paris, 1839).

The first of our forefathers who settled in the county Louth was Neill Gallier, who came from the county Fermanagh, in company with a man called Ruddy; in 1686, they rented the greater part of the lands of Proleek from Robert, the father of Malcolm M' Neale, being a portion of the estate of Ballymascanlon, on which stands the ancient *Cromlech*, or druidical altar — a huge boulder set on three slender vertical stones, by which that place is distinguished; they employed those lands as a stock farm for many years.

Neill Gallier, born in 1646 and died in 1740, at the age of ninety four years, left four sons, Thaddeus, born in 1682 and died in 1783, aged one hundred and one years; his other sons were Terence, Daniel, and Edward.

Thaddeus had six sons, Patrick, born in 1722, died in 1816, aged ninety four ; his other sons were Matthew, Owen, Neill, and John.

Patrick left only one son Thaddeus, born in 1763; this is my venerable father, who is still living.

With the exception of great physical energy, and remarkable longevity, our forefathers could not claim much distinction over their neighbours, if we except a certain loftiness of bearing and a quickness of perception, for which they were generally noted.

My paternal grandfather Patrick was of middle stature and remarkably active; though a sort of jack-of all-trades, his chief occupation was, like that of his father, a dealer in cattle, which they bought in the interior of the Island and prepared for the English market; I remember, when a child the joyous delight in which I loved to place myself between his knees to listen to stories of the fierce encounters he had with wild cattle on his journeyings through the interior and to the wondrous tales of witches and giants, of which he possessed an inexhaustible fund.

Of his wife, Rose Traynor, my grandmother, I can only remember her tall figure and energetic manner; she was very hospitable, and so fond of music that all the strolling minstrels that came her way were sure of a lodging and something to eat.

My grandfather, on the maternal side, was John Taylor, a native of Rosstrevor, county of Down; he was a tall powerful man, and had been a sailor in his youth; after several years passed at sea, with the usual fortunes and vicissitudes of a sailor's life, he returned home with some money, relinquished the sea as a profession, leased a farm near Ballymascanlon, and obtained an appointment in the excise customs at Dundalk, which post he continued to hold as long as he lived.

His wife, Elizabeth Peters, my grandmother, was of Scottish descent — a benevolent and most kindhearted woman, beloved by all who came within her influence; she had a family of two sons and eight daughters, all of whom grew up to maturity, and nearly all left large families; she was not only beloved, but almost worshipped by every one of her grandchildren.

My father, Thaddeus Gallier, was born in Proleek, near the *Cromlech*, and resided during the whole of his long life at that place, or in the village of Ravensdale. He was above the middle height, was blessed with a fine constitution and extraordinary powers of endurance; he possessed a good share of natural ability and mechanical genius, with but slender advantages from education; he had a kindly heart, but a hasty temper; in early life, he had served an apprenticeship to a builder in Dublin, and, on returning to his native home, he married, took a farm, and along with it carried on the business of engineer and builder for more than fifty years; he always gave employment to several mechanics, and had usually three or four apprentices in his establishment. Among other buildings erected by him were the noble mansion of Lord Kilmorey at Mourne Park, and another for Baron Mc Clelland at Ravensdale; he also kept in repair all the dwellings, and machinery of the bleaching mills in the valley for many years; he contrived to get on very comfortably in that manner until about the year 1812, prior to which period the linen trade and bleaching business began to fail, and along with them declined his prosperity and good fortune; for, as at that time the prices of farming produce were upon a war footing very high, he thought he should better his condition by directing exclusive attention to farming; with that view he took upon a short lease a farm at an extravagant rent. This was to all his family the beginning of many troubles; for, when upon the establishment of peace in 1815, the prices of farming produce had fallen to half their former rates, persons like him, who had farms at high rents, were soon reduced to poverty; but time moving onward his lease at length expired, and he got rid of the farm, together with the misery, the losses, and the hard labour it had inflicted upon him and his whole family for several years; the remembrance of those miseries, for many years afterwards, made me shudder whenever farm work was named within my hearing.

Business of every description, as well as farming, suffered great depression at that period, so that my poor father, pressed down as he was by the maintenance of so large a family, could never afterwards attain the prosperous condition he had hitherto enjoyed, though his efforts toward that end, through his subsequent life, had been continuous, but without success.

My mother's maiden name was Margaret Taylor; she was the second child of her parents, and having married at the age of seventeen, brought my father a family of nine sons and four daughters, of whom I was the second born; there had been a daughter before me who died in infancy. My poor dear mother's life was an arduous one, constantly occupied in keeping her children in good condition, and providing for their manifold requirements; she was one of the most kindhearted of women, and if I have ever possessed any goodness of disposition, I inherited it from her; she had excellent judgment in matters of business, and would have kept my father out of many mistakes and troubles had he strictly followed her advice.

She would have shown taste and genius in literary pursuits had she enjoyed proper opportunities for their cultivation; but she died under the age of fifty, worn out by the cares of her numerous family.

My earliest recollection is of being taught at my mother's knee the spelling of simple words; I have no remembrance of learning the alphabet, though I can call to mind things that happened to me when I was not much over three years old.

Of my Birth.

I was born at the village of Ravensdale, in the county of Louth, on the 24th of July, 1798, in one of the most pleasant valleys on the eastern coast of Ireland. The old village had for many years been steadily increasing in the number of its inhabitants, by the many strangers at-

tracted there from all quarters to the bleaching establishments that extended along its river; scarcely one
third the number of cottages or of inhabitants that then
enlivened the valley can be found there at present; but,
however painful it may be to witness such decadency,
the village is much improved in every other respect by
the liberality and taste of its present noble proprietor;
the greater number of the old cottages having been taken
down and replaced by others built on a much improved
plan, while an excellent public school and a good dis-
pensary have been established in the village. It was particularly gratifyng to me, after an absence of thirty years,
to find the old house in which I first saw the light among
the few still left standing.

Besides the mansions of Lord Clearmount and of Baron McClelland, there were other good houses in the
valley belonging to persons who owned the bleaching
grounds that extended along the margin of the river, as
it wound its way from Flurry Bridge towards the bay of
Dundalk. These houses are still there, but the cottages
and the bleaching greens occupied by so many active
peasants have disappeared along with the linen trade
that, up to that period, had insured prosperity to all
who then occupied that happy valley.

Of my School Days.

At the age of about four years I was sent to a small
country school, the only one in the neighbourhood,
which was kept by a poor old Englishman called Brett,
who with a wife and children occupied a miserable cot-
tage of one apartment, that served for " kitchen, for par-
lour, and all" as well as for the school; the scholars were
but few, and we spent the greater part of our time play-

ing all sorts of pranks and games, making little progress in learning, but much in the exercises of running, leaping and wrestling, and we thus grew up as active and hardy as mountain goats.

My brother John was my junior by only twenty months; he and I grew up together in the closest intimacy and brotherly affection. This continued even after we married and had settled separately in life, and it still so continues in a great degree to the present day. My other brothers being several years younger than John and I, we never knew them so intimately as he and I have known each other. After having passed the greater part of six years under Brett, and had learned to read, write, and the first rudiments of arithmetic, we were sent to a school at Dundalk which was kept by the Rev. Samuel Nielson, an excellent man, and a good teacher; but, being then for the first time forced to observe regular habits of study, we were so fretted and annoyed that our health would probably have suffered had we not been forced to walk nearly five miles to school and the same distance back every day. Having thus sufficient exercise for boys of nine or ten years old, we grew up strong and active, fearing no vicissitudes of weather, and making in the main good progress in our studies; but, after two or three years passed in this manner, my father having become involved in those difficulties before related, we were taken from school and were kept to work on the farm, except in the summer months, when we were again sent to school. In this way I continued until I had reached my fourteenth year, at which time the amount of my learning was very small: a smattering of English grammar and composition, arithmetic, and mensuration. I was then taken finally from school, just at the time when I could have made the most rapid progress in studies of any kind, and bound apprentice to my father, to learn the business of a builder; and, as at that time I was living in a country-place without books or the acquaintance of any one of literary tastes or habits, I soon forgot much of the little I had learned at school and my mind lay fallow for several years afterwards.

Shortly after the expiration of my father's lease, there was no employment to be had at his business anywhere about the country, and, as trade of every kind languished or was wholly suspended for the time, the prospects ahead were very unpromising ; it was therefore arranged, chiefly at the suggestion of my mother, that I should go to Dublin and study the art of architectural drawing ; so with that intent my father accompanied me to the city and got me admitted to the School of Fine Arts, which was at that time kept in Hawkens' street. The architectural school was open only on three days of the week, and then for only two hours of each day, so that I had all the intermediate time at my own disposal, and I obtained employment as a builder at some houses that were being erected by Alderman Thorp in Mountjoy's square ; the wages I there received were very small, and, as my father at that time could afford me but little assistance from home, I had to manage very closely to make ends meet.

Having always shown something of a taste for and a strong inclination towards works of art, I now filled up every spare hour I could get at copying the orders of architecture and such other details as I could find at the academy; and, although there was but very little instruction given at the school, I there got the first glimpse of the way in which drawings were made ; and, in the few months passed at that establishment I received the only direct teaching I have ever had.

After having been in Dublin for several months, and Thorpe's buildings being finished, as no further prospect of employment appeared in view, I returned home and was received by my dear mother and all the family with as much kindness and affection as if I had been absent for years.

My father having had some business on hand at that time which employed us for several months, I remained until it was finished, and then, as the prospect at home was unpromising, I concluded to visit England, there seek employment and see something of the country. In the month of May, 1816, I crossed the channel from Dundalk to Liverpool, which was then a very different undertaking from what it is at present in the comfortable steamers engaged in that trade. In 1816, it was no unusual thing to be from three to six days in making the passage across to Liverpool with unfavourable winds.

On my arrival I was told that Manchester promised a better prospect for employment, so I without delay set out to walk from Liverpool, and on reaching Manchester I was employed at the building of a cotton mill, of which there were then but few in existence; my wages were but four shillings per day, which then appeared to me most liberal, and I remained in Manchester as long as I could get employment. I then returned to Liverpool, where I obtained work from a relation of mine who had some years previously served an apprenticeship to my father; I remained with him for several months and then returned home, where I undertook to build a water-wheel for a man who was setting up a spade-foundry at Ravensdale. When that was finished, I engaged to do the joiners' work of a house for a man called Bradford, at Flurry Bridge, which gave me occupation for nine months, having John with me a portion of that time.

The difficulties I encountered in procuring employment about that period were very great; there was no business doing anywhere about the neighbourhood, until in 1818 I was called on to make a plan for and superintend the building of a small country-house for a gentleman at Claret Rock, which kept me engaged for more than a year. My father having then been required to build some additions to the mansion of Lord Kilmorey at Mourne Park, thither John and I went with some other builders, where we were engaged for nine months; after which I was employed to put a new roof upon the Chapel of Grange, at Cooley.

In the autumn of 1820, seeing no prospect of business for the winter, I thought the best use I could make of the time was to try and improve my education, which up to that period had been much neglected; so with that intent I passed several months at a school in Dundalk, where I applied myself assiduously to studies such as bookkeeping, geometry, French and English exercises, etc., etc., and made such general use of those months, as to benefit me very materially in after life.

My father having been about that period appointed to collect the county taxes, he took me with him to assist in their collection, but finding it a very irksome and disagreeable occupation, for which my tastes or habits in no way fitted me, I therefore got rid of it as soon as I was able.

In 1821 and 1822, I obtained some small building contracts about the country, but as they were paltry and unprofitable John and I decided upon going to London and there try our fortunes together at the fountain head. Having procured a letter of introduction to an architect in London, we bade adieu to the family, and to our dear mother, whom we never saw again, as she died within two years of that time.

We took a passage for Liverpool, where we arrived in due time; but, the day after our landing, while walking along a street which had a dead wall on one side, we were alarmed by an accident which might have cut short our travels at the outset; on the inner side of the wall was a paviour's yard, where a quantity of stones were piled up, the pressure of which caused the wall to fall into the street, just the moment after we had passed the spot. This incident caused us great alarm, and gave us food for much serious reflection for many days afterwards. We pushed on to Manchester without delay, where we agreed that if John could get work he would remain, while I should find out whether employment was to be obtained for us in London; and John having got work, I set out alone for the metropolis, where I arrived on the second of July, 1822. On the following day I called on Mr. Wilkins, the architect, and presented my letter of introduction; he received me kindly, and advised me to seek employment from some of the builders about the city, and said that, if I remained in London a sufficient length of time to improve my knowledge of business, he might have it in his power to place me as a *clerk of the works* to some building in the country; I expressed my grateful thanks, and begged permission to leave with him my address as soon as I should have got work and be settled in a lodging. I then withdrew, in very low spirits on finding myself wandering about an utter stranger in that overgrown city. I walked about for several days, staring at all the strange sights that met my view and calling at the yards of several builders, until I at last obtained an engagement from a Mr. Griffiths, of Coleman street, in the city. I then wrote for John, who soon joined me and obtained employment also, but at another place.

About two months before leaving home I had had the misfortune to receive a kick from a horse upon the leg, and was laid up for several weeks. The wound got better; but, when I arrived in London, the weather being hot, from constantly walking or standing, the leg began to inflame and soon became so bad that I had to repose for some weeks at my lodging. As the limb still grew worse, I was advised to apply for admission into Guy's Hospital; though I very much disliked the idea of entering it, I applied, and after several efforts was at last admitted under the care of Doctor Lucas, who at first had fears that I should lose the leg; after some weeks, however, it took a favourable turn and began to mend, so that in ten weeks after my admission I was able to walk about again. I then obtained work with John at the establishment of Messrs. Cover and Lawrence, builders, in Pitfield street, Hoxton.

In a short time after we had become acquainted with the London methods of doing business, we took piece-work from our employers, and being very strong and active were soon able to save some money, and nearly the first few pounds we had saved we sent home to the family in Ireland. In our second year in London we entered into a new arrangement with our employers, by which we agreed to take large quantities of joiners' work at certain fixed prices, and then engaged other men to assist us in its execution; this we continued to do for nearly three years, and managed to lay by a little money. There were several other young and active workmen in the shop with us engaged at piecework, and exerting ourselves to the utmost we soon became so expert as to accomplish twice as much in a day as men usually did in shops where the piecework system did not prevail.

Having previously to leaving Ireland become acquainted with an amiable young English girl, Miss Elizabeth Tyler, whose parents resided near Market-Drayton, in Shropshire, we maintained a correspondence for some time and now agreed to marry; so with that intent I made a journey from London into Shropshire in the month of January, 1823, met her at her father's house, and was shortly after married. We immediately afterwards returned to London, where I resumed my former employment along with John at the establishment of Cover and Lawrence.

In the following year John married also; but we continued together in the same employment for two years longer, when with the view of bettering our circumstances we opened a small place of business on our own account; but, notwithstanding our utmost efforts, the speculation failed to realise our expectations. We did not then understand that young men without friends have but slender chances of success in setting up for themselves a business like ours in such a place as London.

During the greater part of my stay in London I devoted every spare hour to the study of the higher principles of the art of building. I carefully studied the works of Nicholson, Tredgold, and others on the science of construction, the strength of materials, etc.; read all the works I could procure upon engineering, the steam-engine, and machinery; also those upon the principles of architecture and the fine arts.

Having as before stated left my address with **Mr. Wilkins**, I was in 1826 favoured with a letter from him, saying that, if I still felt a desire to be engaged as a *clerk of the works*, he had something in view which might suit me; and if I would meet him at the town of Huntingdon, he could there point out the duties I should have to perform if I entered into the engagement. I attended at the appointed time and place, and found he was about to build a prison for the county of Huntingdon. Having examined into my fitness for the situation, he engaged me at a salary of four pounds per week, to take charge of the plans, and to see that the work was performed by the contractor in accordance with the drawings and specification.

I was highly delighted with my new situation, being the first employment I ever had that held out a prospect of advancing my position in life; so, having returned to London and put my affairs in order, I took my family down to Huntingdon and soon had everything put into proper working condition.

In a year after marriage our first child was born, which was a boy, but he died in early infancy; our second was a girl, who lived to the age of four years; our third was my dear son James, the only one now left; he was born at Huntingdon on the 25th of September, 1827, and was christened in the picturesque old church of that town; our fourth was a girl, born after our return to London, but died in early childhood.

My next neighbour at Huntingdon was Mr. Robert Carruthers, a literary man, who carried on the business of a bookbinder at the same time with the management of the county school. He published a history of Huntingdon and other works; and, having afterwards removed to Scotland, became the editor and ultimately the proprietor of the " Inverness Courier, " which he has conducted with great ability for many years. This excellent man was of much service to me : he directed me to a course of reading and put me in the way of obtaining the use of books. I became a member of a debating society and of a social club; I also joined a masonic lodge, and, during the two years of my stay at Huntingdon, my knowledge of life and of the ways of society became much enlarged.

I made a small wooden model of the gaol, so constructed that the roofs and the upper storeys could be separately lifted up to show the interior divisions of all the yards, passages, rooms, and cells throughout the building; this I sent to Mr. Wilkins, who was highly pleased with it.

I was frequently called on by persons of the town and neighbourhood of Huntingdon to give plans for alterations to their houses; I also planned and superintended the erection of a small wooden bridge, of an original design, across a branch of the river Ouse at Godmanchester, and I now began to fancy myself a person of some little importance. To understand the degree of elation I at that time felt, a man must have started in in life as I had done, on nearly the lowest rung of the social ladder, and have toiled his way painfully upward, even to the very humble position I had then attained.

The building of the prison having been at length completed, I received an encouraging offer to return to London and superintend the building of a range of houses in South street, near Park lane, agreeably to plans made by Mr. John Deering, architect; I accepted the offer, and returned to London with my family in June, 1828. Having now in London the advantage of consulting the principal writers on the arts in general and on architecture in particular, I applied myself assiduously to study, and before my engagement at those houses had terminated, I was employed by several persons about that quarter of London to furnish plans for new buildings and alterations to old ones.

I clearly perceived, however, that though I might in time succeed in a small way and to a limited extent, I could never reckon upon any great success in London without the patronage of people in high station; and as with such people I had no influence, I saw it was hopeless to expect much success in that direction.

But having heard that any person well acquainted with the practice of building, as well as having a fair knowledge of architecture as an art, could scarcely fail of success in the United States of America, I therefore came to the conclusion that *there* lay the proper field for my labours.

Not having seen my native home in Ireland for ten years, I made a visit to my father and relations before setting out for the New World.

On my return to London I soon made the necessary preparations for crossing the Atlantic, and left the St. Catherine's docks on the eighth of February, 1832, on board an American ship called the Louisiana. We had a tedious and stormy voyage of sixty five days, but landed safely in New York : a wintry voyage across the Atlantic was in those days a very different affair from what it is at present.

I left my wife and family in London to reside with John and his family, and set out alone as pioneer to find in what part of America I was most likely to meet with a desirable place to make a settlement.

On my arrival at New York on the 14 th of April, 1832, I considered a large city as the most likely place to expect employment in my profession, but here I found that the majority of the people could with difficulty be made to understand what was meant by a professional architect; the builders, that is, the carpenters and bricklayers, all called themselves architects, and were at that time the persons to whom owners of property applied when they required plans for building; the builder hired some poor draftsman, of whom there were some half a dozen in New York at that time, to make the plans, paying him a mere trifle for his services. The drawings so made were, it is true, but of little value, and some proprietors built without having any regular plan. When they wanted a house built, they looked about for one already finished, which they thought suitable to their purpose; and then bargained with a builder to erect for them such another, or one with such alterations upon the model as they might point out. All this was soon changed, however, and architects began to be employed by proprietors before going to the builders; and in this way, in a short time, the style of buildings public and private showed signs of rapid improvement.

There was at that time, properly speaking, only one architect's office in New York, kept by Town and Davis. Town had been a carpenter, but was no draftsman; he had obtained a patent for a wooden bridge, the *right* to erect which he sold to several parties in the States, and had made some money by it; he had been once or twice to London, and bought there a large collection of books in various languages upon the arts, and furnished his office with a very respectable library, which he afterwards, as I was told, bequeathed to Yale College, at New-Haven. Davis, his partner, was no mechanic, but was a good draftsman, and possessed much taste as an artist; he had furnished the plans for many of the public buildings in some of the States of that time.

There was a Mr. Dakin, a young man of genius, who had been a carpenter and had studied architecture in Town's office; at the time of my arrival, he had opened an office of his own, where he made drawings for the builders; from him I obtained the first employment I had in America; and as he found me much better acquainted with business in general than any of the draftsmen at that time in New York, he proposed to employ me at four dollars per day; so I went into his office and remained there for several months.

As soon as I had thus procured employment I wrote for my wife and son, who with John and his family came out and joined me at New York, in the month of July, 1832. The Asiatic cholera had by that time made its first appearance in America, and committed dreadful havoc in New York, but few families having wholly escaped it; ours fortunately did so, however, as we went into the country until the violence of the epidemic had abated.

There was at that time in New York a draftsman called Lafever, who had been in the employment of a builder; he came to me and proposed to join me as a partner in opening an architect's office; he said he had an extensive connection of influential friends, who would patronise us in business.

After some consideration I agreed to his proposal, and we opened an office in Clinton Hall, where we obtained from the builders orders for as many drawings as we could well make; but I found it very disagreeable work, and so badly rewarded, that I began to cast about and see if there was no other way by which I could improve my situation, and escape from this horse-in-a-mill routine of grinding out drawings for the builders.

Perceiving that there was no such thing as a *Builder's Price Book* at New-York, I fancied that if I published one upon a plan similar to that of London, it might, if not profitable, be at least the means of making my name known among the builders throughout the country : I therefore set to work, and in four months produced the *"American Builder's Price Book."* As a speculation I only lost money by it, but indirectly it was of much service to me. To show with what energy I strove to get forward, at that period I got up a course of lectures on architecture, with illustrative drawings, which I read a few times in public, but with no other advantage than that of making my name better known among the people.

It was then intimated to me by persons who had been to the south, that New Orleans would be a much better place for me to settle in than New York, if I could only bear the climate; for, though mercantile men went down there from the north every year, they generally remained during the winter months only, and returned northward in the summer to escape the yellow fever ; this they continued to do until they had in some degree become acclimatised; but an architect could not do this; he must remain all the summer from his first beginning, as that was the season when buildings were chiefly erected at New Orleans.

Lafever and I having then dissolved our copartnership, I left with him the collection of various outstanding debts due to our firm, but of which I never received any part from him afterwards.

Having determined to run the hazard of New Orleans, I prepared without delay to go there, and make a trial, leaving my family in the meantime at New York : so that, in October, 1834, I set off by sea, accompanied by a young man, a brother of the Mr. Dakin before mentioned.

We landed at Mobile, where we remained a few weeks, until the yellow fever had for that season disappeared from New Orleans; we then went there, and hired an office on Canal street, hung its walls with plans and drawings, and began to look out for something to do.

The corporation of the city of Mobile having decided upon building a Town Hall, advertised for plans, and we made a design for it which obtained the first prize of three hundred dollars; though but a trifle, it served to place our names before the public : but in consequence of a fire, by which a large portion of Mobile was destroyed, the Hall was never built. We made plans for a church, and for a public school, which were erected there, and are still the most important-looking buildings in Government street.

A company having been at that time formed for erecting a large hotel in New Orleans, which was afterwards named the "Saint Charles." The owner of the ground, Mr. John Hagan, was president of the company; he, as well as several of the chief shareholders were Irish merchants, who had been established in business there for many years; these gentlemen welcomed me as a country-man, and treated me with great kindness. I made a design for the new hotel, which gave general satisfaction; the committee adopted it, and engaged me to superin-tend its erection. I demanded for my services a per-cen-tage upon the cost of the building as was usual in such cases in England; but to this they would not consent, but finally agreed to pay me ten thousand dollars for the plans, drawings, and superintendence. As all the stone work, the greater part of the joiners' work and iron work, had at that time to be prepared at the north, involving a vast amount of drawing and writing, and as the time required for the erection extended over a space of three years, the amount of compensation was not nearly as much as it should have been; but I gained reputation by it, which brought in other business that paid better.

The soil of the lower part of Louisiana being wholly alluvial, intermingled with the trunks and roots of old trees which had for ages been brought down by the Mississippi river and deposited along its margin, may be literally said to be afloat, as water every-where in the vicinity of New Orleans is found at a foot or two below the surface of the ground when the river is high; this causes much trouble with heavy buildings, as the walls sink down to a depth proportioned to their height. The only way to prevent unequal settlement is to make the *width* of the foundations commensurate with the *height* of the walls and the *weight* which each wall will have to bear; the deeper the foundation is dug, the less capable will it be to support superincumbent weight. I found the best way was to expand the base of the foundations in proportion to the intended height of the walls. For the hotel, I had reckoned on a foot and a half for sinking, but as it continued to go down for five years after it was built, it sunk a foot more than I had allowed before it finally stopped. The progress of the building was much retarded the first summer by the number of deaths that occurred among the workmen from sun stroke or yellow fever; the loss of life from these causes was truly appalling. In addition to this source of trouble I was forced to act not only as the architect, but also as clerk of the works and foreman mechanic in each of the trades engaged in the building, as the only men who could at that time be had knew little or nothing of building beyond the most common structures, I had therefore to direct every movement in each department, by which my employment became very arduous and onerous.

The hotel was finished in 1836, and when completed had entrances from three different streets; the principal one was on St. Charles street. The basement story consisted of shops and offices which were rented to various occupants. The principal entrances were gained by a flight of granite steps at each end of a projecting platform, on which stood a Corinthian portico, having an inner range of columns, with a deep recess behind them, where the entrance doors were placed.

In the centre of the structure was an octagonal building, which, extending above the roofs, was terminated by a circular order of columns, and surmounted by a dome that produced a fine effect, and could be seen at a great distance from every side on approaching the city. In the basement story of the octagon was placed the bar-room, where an extensive counter was constantly supplied with various kinds of eatables, furnished gratis to any one who chose to pay for one of those drinks or compounds for which American bar-rooms are celebrated; many a "Man about town" lived nearly altogether at this, or at other bar-rooms, and frequently cut short his life by habits of intemperance, first acquired and afterwards kept up by establishments of this description.

On the principal store were placed the dining rooms, the saloons, the private parlours, and the drawing rooms; the kitchens and all the working parts of the establishment, as well as the bathing rooms, were situated in the back wing; there were rooms to lodge and accommodate nearly five hundred people, and the hotel, taken as a whole, was acknowledged by all who then saw it to be the most complete and beautiful structure of the kind that had up to that period been erected in America.

During my first summer in New Orleans, besides the St. Charles Hotel, I was engaged to furnish plans for and superintend the building of a merchants' exchange on Royal street, which was afterwads converted into the Post-office; the design for the dome and roof over the large room was somewhat peculiar and caused a good deal of criticism among the builders : there was a Mr. Nicholls, who had for some time previously been the state architect and engineer; he pronounced that the building, if constructed according to my design, would be insecure and the dome could not stand. The building committee, on hearing this, desired me to have the plans altered, but I refused to do this, and invited Mr. Nicholls to discuss the safety of the design scientifically in presence of the committee; but as he declined to do so, I drew up a statement showing in detail, on principles laid down by Tredgold and others, that every part of the construction had been carefully considered and duly provided for : the committee were satisfied, and desired me to go on with the work, which I did; everything was finished in due time, and has remained firm and secure to the present day. My reputation having gained some advantage by this discussion, I soon had applications from other parties for as many plans and contracts as I could possibly attend to.

Having passed through the summer of 1835 without taking the yellow fever, I thought all danger from it for that year had gone by, when late in November, having been much exposed to the weather on a damp cold day, I was in the evening seized by a chill fit, followed by violent fever; a doctor was sent for, who bled me profusely; he returned next day bringing another doctor with him, and bled me again; they then considered my case a very perilous one and called in a third; and the three continued to visit me three times a day to the sixth night, by which time the disease had reached a crisis and I became delirious, but on the following morning the fever had subsided and I was then so feeble that I could not move a muscle nor make my voice heard. By the several bleedings, cuppings, and leechings it was computed that I had in four days lost ninety six ounces of blood, and had taken nearly one hundred grains of calomel in one dose; this produced an effect which everything else had failed to do. That was one of the methods adopted in the treatment for yellow fever in those days; but every year the fever assumed a different type, and required a different mode of treatment; it was only by observing the greatest care and prudence that I was enabled to leave my room at the end of three weeks, after the fever had left me.

During my illness, the building committee of the hotel

devoted to me the most unceasing attention; nothing that care or physic could accomplish was left undone, and to this circumstance I chiefly attributed my recovery.

On resuming business again I found myself overwhelmed by difficulties in procuring the services of good workmen to carry out the various contracts I had in hand : I found that mechanics who understood their business, even only tolerably well, preferred taking small contracts on their own account to working for others, so that those who were to be had for hire knew little or nothing of their business, and required constant supervision and instruction. I had at the time a foreman carpenter who was a very good mechanic; but he, then taking advantage of the circumstances, told me he had received an offer from a man who was long established in business to be taken in as a partner, but that he would prefer remaining with me, if I offered him a similar arrangement; otherwise, he must leave me. Situated as I then was, I felt myself compelled to agree to the terms of his demand; so I took him in as a partner, having one-third interest in the building department of my business, but not in the architectural. He remained with me for three years, but disputes and bickerings having frequently arisen between us, we agreed to separate, and I was made happy on finding myself once again the sole master of my own affairs.

I then engaged as foreman a young Englishman who had been a stairbuilder in my employment for some time previously : he made an excellent foreman, was a most trustworthy person in every way, and remained with me as long as I continued in business.

I also engaged as bookkeeper a most estimable young

man who had been brought up in the office of a wine-merchant in London; he was intelligent and worthy of all confidence; so that he also remained with me as long as I continued in business.

At the solicitation of my architectural partner, Mr. Charles Dakin, his brother James came from New York in 1835, and they proposed that he should join us as a partner in the office; but I doubted whether three of us could agree together in such a business as ours; I therefore proposed to withdraw and leave the office to them, stipulating, however, that as the St. Charles Hotel and the Post-office were exclusively my own designs, I should continue to superintend them until completed; we separated upon these conditions. I paid over to Charles his proportion of what had been received by us from the commencement, and I left with them all the unfinished business in the office. They continued to practice there successfully for a year or two, when Charles removed to and opened a branch office at Mobile, where among other business he made a contract to build a range of brick stores and warehouses; but, whether from the want of sufficient experience as a builder or proper care in the construction, the whole range of buildings tumbled down while the roofs were being put on: this misfortune so preyed upon the spirits of the poor fellow, that, happening to take a severe cold, a rapid disease of the lungs followed, which carried him off in little more than a year.

Having by that time bought some lots of ground fronting on Common and Carondelet streets in New Orleans, I there established my office and workshops, and occupied them as such as long as I remained in business.

A plan having been made by Dakin for a new Catholic church in Camp street, he was employed by the committee to superintend its erection; but, when the walls of the building had reached nearly to the roof, a disagreement between Dakin and the managers took place, and he withdrew from the undertaking. After much delay, the managers employed me to finish the structure; but before the walls of the tower had risen above the roof, they began to settle down toward one side, from a defective foundation; so that I had to take out the old foundation and put in a new one, without pulling down the walls; this caused much trouble and expense, but I finally succeeded in accomplishing it, so that it has stood firmly to the present day.

The whole of the interior arrangements, the groined ceilings, the altar, the organ, etc., were erected after my designs and under my superintendence.

I had been much embarrassed for some time in procuring timber for the various buildings I had in hand; the sawmills were few in number, and the demands upon them so great, that buildings were often much delayed from this cause. Mr. Thomas Barrett, a well-known merchant of the city, and president of a bank, had a sawmill at Lafayette where I was in the habit of getting much of the timber required for my contracts, wanting to dispose of this mill, proposed to sell it to me, and took much pains in pointing out the many advantages I should derive from having full command of the establishment.

There were two men who had for some years conducted the business of the mill for him: the one, called Walsh, was the manager; the other, called Burdon, was the bookkeeper; both lived upon the premises; and

Barrett, giving them excellent characters, strongly advised that I should join with them in the business of the mill and in the purchase of the property on which it stood, and to allow them a liberal salary for managing the business. I took the advice of some friends upon it, and in an unlucky hour I decided upon entering into the speculation.

The property consisted of three squares of ground, twenty-five negroes, a stock of horses, mules, etc.; the sawmill, with steam engine and machinery, all in toler-ably good working condition; the price was one hundred and forty thousand dollars; for which we gave jointly our promissory notes, bearing interest at six per cent. per annum, payable by instalments extending over five years; and, had my partners acted honestly in the business, it would have been a profitable speculation for all concerned in it. During the first six months the profits amounted to twenty thousand dollars, and every thing went on very hopefully; but for the next six months the profits did not much exceed half that sum: Walsh and Burdon accounted for this great falling off by saying the machinery was growing old and required frequent repairs, by which the work was retarded; at the end of every succeeding six months the apparent profits kept regularly diminishing, though the mill was in full operation; and as the profits no longer sufficed to liquidate the notes given for the property as they became due, the interest upon them was accumulating, and the firm was rapidly drifting into debt. I frequently, along with my bookkeeper, examined the books of the firm, but after the most rigid investigation, no errors were discovered by which I could prove, though I strongly suspected, nefarious practices by the managing partners. Things went on in this way for a space of three years, at the end of which time, Burdon was killed by being accidentally thrown from his gig. Walsh then evinced the greatest alarm upon finding that of thirty thousand dollars worth of landed property bought by Burdon for himself and Walsh conjointly, in the course of those three years, the whole appeared to stand exclusively in the name of Burdon, and Walsh could show no title to any part of it; so that, with the view of trying to recover some portion of it, he produced several memorandum books that had been kept by Burdon, and were filled with entries of lots of timber sold by him to various persons for cash at the mill, but of which he had entered no part in the books of the firm; this accounted for my inability to discover their frauds by examining the books. Walsh pretended to have just discovered these memorandums among Burdon's private papers, and said he was until then wholly unacquainted with their existence, and now proposed that I should join him in a suit against Burdon's estate, for restitution of the funds of which he had swindled the firm. Being convinced, however, that both one and the other had been equally concerned in the fraud, I first of all secured those memorandums, placed them in court for safe keeping, and then entered suit against the estates of Walsh and Burdon in solido for the amount of what they had cheated me.

As soon as Walsh found me determined to sue him, he made simulated sales of all the property that had anywhere stood in his name, including a cotton plantation, to a cousin of his who lived upon the plantation at some distance up the river. He then commenced an energetic defence against my suit, to prevent a judgment from being recorded against him for the space of two years from the *date* of the sales, as by a law of Louisiana, a sale could not be set aside after two year's had elapsed from its *date*, excepting where a judgment from a court could be recorded against it before the end of that time. So that, when I had at last obtained a judgment for sixty thousand dollars against Walsh and Burdon, it was too late, for no property belonging to Walsh could then be found that I could legally touch; and as for Burdon's estate, so many privileged creditors appeared that very little of it was left for any one.

Walsh, having then retired to his plantation, demanded from his cousin a reconveyance of the property with which he had intrusted him; but this the latter refused to do; the property stood now in his name, and he said he intended to keep it so. On this, Walsh became perfectly furious; he lost all self-control, took to drinking brandy, went about with a bottle in his pocket, and a gun on his arm, in a state of absolute frenzy, awaiting the re-appearance of his cousin who had fled from the plantation. After several days passed in this manner, Walsh suddenly disappeared; but within a week a body was found floating in the river, about sixty miles below the plantation, which on being examined proved to be that of Walsh shot through the heart by a charge of buck shot; his cousin was suspected of the murder, but as no proof could be adduced against him he was permitted to go at large. Such was the end of those two men by whom I had been cheated and robbed in so villanous a manner, and adds one more proof to the truth, of the saying, that "honesty is the best policy."

Having at length obtained exclusive possession of the sawmill and its appendages, I tried energetically to clear off the debts with which it was encumbered, and was making satisfactory progress when the mill took fire and was totally burnt down. I fortunately nad it insured for two-thirds of its value; and I now consulted the holders of the mortgage notes upon it as to the most prudent course to be pursued. I proposed to sell the whole property by auction in separate lots, the proceeds of which, along with the amount insured, ought to clear off all the debts upon it. The creditors agreed to this. I caused a sale to be made of everything belonging to it, paid off the claims against me, and after infinite trouble got clear of the unfortunate speculation, which had absorbed the produce of a lucrative business for ten of the best years of my life, between the ages of thirty-five and forty-five years.

I set to work again with renewed energy, if not a wiser, a more prudent man; and in the course of years succeeded in realising sufficient property for the supply of all reasonable wants.

In the autumn of 1836 my wife and son came to me from New York, with John and his family, and remained with me during the winter; but as soon as the hot weather of summer set in, my wife and son both became so ill that the doctors advised their departure for the north. John and his family were also equally anxious to go northward : they had not prospered in New Orleans, for while in the winter he was visiting a planing machine his foot was caught by the machinery, and so much injured as to keep him on crutches for several months. They, therefore, all set off together by sea for New York, where John and his family have continued to reside to the present time.

My wife having taken up her residence at New York concluded to remain there and attend to the care and the education of our only son; who was, after a year or two, sent to an institute established on Long Island by the Reverend Doctor Hawks, and there remained with few intermissions until that establishment was closed in 1843.

While engaged at building the St. Charles Hotel, I made several contracts for building houses and stores for various other parties, and then introduced the system of ten hours' labour for a day's work ; this was hailed by the men as a great amelioration, as the custom up to that time had been to work from sunrise to sunset, which was very distressing to the men in the hot days of summer, without, upon the whole, producing any greater amount of work. I also established another custom, that of paying every man the full amount of his wages at the end of every second week. By these means I acquired so much popularity, that I could always command the services of the best men in each department, and by thus accomplishing a greater amount of business in a given time, of better quality and with less trouble to myself, than could any other builder at that time in the city. I *let* out the brickwork, stone work, plastering, painting, slating, and ironwork, to persons already established in those several trades, and I made it a practice to employ the same people, when possible, in each department, as long as I remained in business. I mention these particulars for the purpose of showing how I was enabled to conduct so large a business with so few assistants as I at any time had with me, and especially in such a climate as that of New Orleans.

While living in London, where every inch of building ground is turned to the best account, I had some experience in contriving to make the most of small spaces, and I now turned this knowledge to good advantage. There were three gentlemen who owned, among them, one lot of ground of no very great extent, and consulted

3

me as to the best mode of improving it. One of them said in a jocular way *he* should like three good houses built upon it. I took the hint, and made a plan for three houses, which appeared so feasible that they made a contract with me to build them, and when finished the owners expressed the highest satisfaction, and called them the " three sisters. "

There was a merchant of New Orleans, who, after many years in trade, had succeeded in realising a handsome fortune, and proposed to retire from business ; but previous to doing so, he wished to complete a certain round sum , and for that purpose purchased a large quantity of cotton, which he shipped off for Liverpool ; before it reached that port, however, a sudden fall in price had taken place, so that instead of the large profit he had anticipated, he lost the whole amount of his capital and became a bankrupt. A short time before this unfortunate speculation , he had entered into a contract with me to build him a house on Esplanade street ; the house was finished, and possession of it delivered when his misfortune came upon him ; and I lost over two thousand dollars by him and it.

The gasworks company, requiring a large chimney, had three chimneys in succession erected upon the same spot, which had all failed ; they had either fallen down, or had to be pulled down, for the want of proper foundations ; the ground being but a swamp of water and soft mud, interspersed with the roots and trunks of old trees that had for ages been carried down by the river and deposited there, and had at last attained a depth of nearly a hundred feet.

The company employed me to plan and superintend the building of a new chimney on a much larger scale ;

one that I could guarantee to stand. I gave it a much more extensive base to stand on, dug out the mud to a considerable depth, filled the space with piles driven as deeply as possible, and made up the interstices with concrete, on which the brick foundation, built in hydraulic cement, was laid. It was a costly work of the kind, but it has stood firmly, and has answered the purpose very completely.

The waterworks company had a large basin built in four compartments, erected upon a mound which was composed of the mud deposited by the river; but the walls of the basin were so badly constructed that no greater depth than about two feet of water could be safely contained in them, though a depth of five feet was required to supply the city. The managing committee advertised for plans by which the walls could be so secured as to render them capable of sustaining the requisite quantity of water.

This brought out a variety of contrivances, some of which were curious, while others were quite ridiculous. An Italian engineer maintained that the winds blowing across the basin produced waves that shook and detroyed the walls; he seriously demonstrated his theory, and proposed as a remedy the construction of a series of brick piers to stand within the basin, which would act as *wind breakers*. This idea produced a good deal of merriment among the committee.

I proposed to place a series of iron bars round the outside of the basin, with diagonal tie-rods within, so as to give the walls a counterbalancing support in every direction.

My plan was approved, and, since the work was finished, the basins have answered all the purposes required very effectually.

Several years before I reached New Orleans, plans and instructions had been sent from Washington to build a branch Mint, and the construction of the building was confided to a carpenter and a bricklayer of the city. The floors were sustained upon groined brick arches, supported by square brick pillars; but the thrust of the arches having caused the abutments to give way, the arches began to sink at the crown, and the whole structure threatened to become soon a mass of ruin. I was called on in a great hurry to devise some method of averting the danger. I caused to be inserted strong iron rods from outside to outside of the building in each direction; by shoring up the crowns of the arches and tightening up the rods, they having screw knuts and outside plates, the building was rendered perfectly secure, and has remained so to the present time.

In the course of the ten years following 1836 I had made plans for, and built by contract, a great number of private dwellings and stores, for various persons in and about New Orleans, and had I restricted my practice to that description of business, I could have retired with a sufficient competency long before I was enabled to do so. A gentleman calling on me in 1842 stated that while at Havana, whence he had just returned, an agent of Count O'Reilly had requested of him, that, on his return to New Orleans, he would obtain from the architect of the Saint Charles Hotel a plan for a new hotel, which Count O'Reilly intended to have built at Havana. I replied that without a plan of the ground and of the adjoining property I could do nothing. He advised me to go myself to Havana, and

see the count, who would give me all the information I
might require. I asked whether he considered it worth
the trouble to enter upon a business of this kind without
having some certainty of compensation for my time and
expenses. He replied that Count O'Reilly being one of
the richest noblemen of Cuba, he might of course be
relied on for fair dealing in any thing he should under-
take. I therefore decided upon going to Havana, and
when introduced to Count O'Reilly, he received me po-
litely, stated his intention to build a large hotel, and directed his agent to procure all the information I might
desire. Having obtained this, I returned to New
Orleans, made out a full set of plans, and specifications
in English and in Spanish, and an estimate of the whole
cost. Having prepared everything, I set off again for
Havana, where, on my arrival, the agent informed me
that Count O'Reilly was at his plantation in the country,
but would return to town in a few days. It was then
the month of May, the rainy season had set in, and
I remained in Havana for three weeks in the daily ex-
pectation of seeing the count return, but still he did not
appear. The agent then said that the roads had become
so impassable, he could not say *when* the count could
reach the city. He therefore advised me not to remain
any longer at that time, but to leave the plans with him,
and he would present them to the count on his return.
I did not like the idea of leaving the plans in his possession ; so I placed them in the custody of Messrs. Drake
and C^o. with instructions that one thousand dollars should
be placed in their hands for me before possession of
the plans should be given to the count, for by that
time I had heard many unfavourable reports of the
count and of his agent in matters of business.

I returned to New Orleans, and in a short time wrote

to the count respecting the hotel, but he never replied to me. Drake and C°. informed me that on the return of the count they told him they had possession of the plans, and of my instructions as to their delivery; that the count told them he had changed his intention of building an hotel, and should therefore not now require the plans at all. After some months had elapsed, they sent me back my plans, and I have never received any compensation for my labours, loss of time, the expenses of two voyages to Havana and back, besides time lost in waiting there for several weeks. I had at one time intended to sue the count for compensation of my claims; but was dissuaded from that course by persons who knew how hopeless a thing it was for a stranger to get any compensation through the medium of the law, or the lawyers at Havana, against a wealthy native with unlimited means of defence.

In the year of 1843, after the closing of Doctor Hawkes' establishment on Long Island, the doctor with his family moved to the state of Mississippi, and there set up an establishment for preparing young men to enter college; thither I sent my son James, where he remained until he entered college at Chapel Hill, North Carolina.

My poor dear wife, whose health was always delicate, came with our son from New York, with the intention of remaining permanently with me at New Orleans. During the winter months she went on tolerably well; but when summer set in her health became very much impaired. I wanted to remove her to a cooler climate, but to this she would not consent without I could accompany her. My business engagements, however, totally preventing this, she decided to remain with me at New Orleans, where in the summer she became so seriously ill, that, after some weeks' suffering under a severe nervous fever, she died in the month of July, 1843, and thus passed away as kind a heart and as pure a spirit as ever animated human clay.

Mr. Thomas Barrett, having been appointed to the collectorship of customs at New Orleans, applied to me for a design for a new custom-house; but being fully occupied at the time I refused having any thing to do with it, without positive assurance of being paid for my trouble. He assured me that as the secretary of the treasury at Washington had requested him to get plans made for it, he would undoubtedly cause a liberal compensation to be paid me for any trouble or labour I might bestow upon it. With this understanding I set to work, and in three months produced two different sets of plans, one for a building being more costly than the other. I placed the drawings and specifications, when finished, in a tin case, which I delivered to Mr. Barrett, who sent it to the treasury department at Washington; but I could gain no information of or concerning it for nearly two years; in the meantime, Mr. Barrett had been superseded in the collectorship by Mr. Denis Prieur. A short time prior to that event, a man of the name of Wood, who had formerly been a builder in New Orleans, but had only recently returned from the state prison at Baton Rouge, where he had passed five years in confinement for the murder of his foreman, was at this time trying to get into business again, and having at a late election made himself conspicuously active in the interest of one of the parties, had by that means acquired the favour and support of that party of which Mr. Prieur, the collector, was a prominent member. Wood, having obtained from the party a letter of recommendation, headed by Mr. Prieur, to the treasury department, with which he went to Washington, and for several months attended assiduously upon the secretary, having free access to all the plans and models that had been sent in, and from them concocted a design in accordance with the taste and ideas of the secretary, who adopted it, and appointed Wood to be the architect and superintendent of the building to the astonishment of all who knew anything of Wood's previous history. I addressed several letters to the treasury department requesting compensation for my plans agreeably to the promises made me by Mr. Barrett ,and for the return of my plans and the model by which they were accompanied. My letters remained unanswered for several months, but I at length received the tin case with the drawings, which were by that time so much soiled and torn as to be unfit to be looked at; but of the model I have never gained any information whatever , and I have never received the slightest compensation for the time and labour expended upon those plans nor for the expenses in travelling to and from Washington on that business.

In 1844 the congregation of Christ's Church, in New Orleans, having invited Doctor Hawkes to be their rector, they sold the old church, and made arrangements to build a new one. The doctor had with him at that time a gentleman who had been the drawing-master at his school, and who had made a sketch design for the new church ; but I had to make so many alterations in the plan, before it could be made practically fit to build from, as to make it amount to a new design. I entered into a contract with the trustees to erect the building, and it was taken possession of by the congregation within two years from its commencement.

In 1845 the building of a Municipal Hall, for the

second district of New Orleans, having been decided on, I was employed to make plans for and to super-intend the erection of the edifice. A contract was entered into with a builder to execute the work, which he went on with under my superintendence until the walls had attained the height of one storey, at which time a stop was put to the work from the want of funds to go on with the building. The contractor then sued and obtained a judgment against the municipality for non-compliance with their part of the contract. When that was settled, the building committee commissioned me to provide the requisite materials and workmen to go on with and finish the building; and this I accomplished in two years, to the satisfaction of all concerned. The design of the roof is peculiar : it is partly of wood and partly of iron, confined to a very flat pitch, spanning over a width of eighty-six feet, and having an arched ceiling and galleries suspended from it underneath. The portico and ashlar of the front are of white marble, procured from quarries near New York; the basement and steps are of granite, the style of the architecture is Grecian Ionic, and the portico is considered as a very chaste and highly-finished example of that style.

In that same year of 1845 a company was formed to build a commercial Exchange to front on Saint Charles street. I made the design for it, and entered into a contract to erect the building. It consisted of one large room on the lower storey, intended for the Exchange; another large and lofty room on the second storey in-tended for lectures, and public exhibitions, and two storeys of rooms on each side for offices. But a public Exchange has never been found to answer at New Or-leans, as the merchants there could not be induced to assemble on change as they do in other cities; it was therefore found necessary in a short time to alter the arrangement of the building, so that the lower storey was converted into stores and offices, while the large room above was used as a masonic lodge; and since that time, the whole building has become the property of the Masonic Society of New Orleans.

In 1846, having some lots of ground adjoining my building yard, I pulled down the old edifices thereon and erected new ones, which I rented out to various tenants, and received from them a handsome income.

During the practice of my profession at New Orleans, I could find no person capable of giving me much assistance in making drawings; I was therefore obliged to do nearly all the drawings myself, so that, by overtaxing my strength, I was brought to such a condition from congestion of the eyes and head, as to be confined to a darkencd chamber for many weeks, and was at last so much reduced by depletion that I had to visit New York and place myself under the care of an oculist, who in three months fortunately succeeded in restoring my sight, and I was thus enabled on my return to New Orleans to resume the practice of my profession. But in 1847 I again found my head congested, and my general health so much impaired that I was advised to visit England and try the cold-water cure; so with that intent I engaged a passage on board a ship from New Orleans to Liverpool. My only fellow-passenger was the Reverend Theodore Clapp, than whom a more agreeable and intelligent companion no one could desire. Our skipper was an old East India captain, an excellent man, possessing an infinite variety of anecdote and information; so that, though the voyage lasted fifty-seven days, it never seemed tedious nor uninteresting, and on landing at Liverpool I found my health much improved by the voyage. I went to Malvern and remained at Doctor Gully's establishment for two months, but did not receive so much benefit from it at that time as I was led to expect.

I then visited Ireland and spent some weeks with my father, whom I had not seen for several years. I returned to Liverpool, and engaged a passage for New York, taking with me a sister's daughter who had been left an orphan. When I arrived at New Orleans I placed her at a ladies' school at Mobile. She afterwards became the wife of Mr. Robert Ferguson, an engineer, at that time in successful practice at New Orleans, but dying a few years afterwards, he left his wife and children in very straitened circumstances.

I actively commenced business again, and kept on at it through the winter; but in the spring finding my health beginning to give way, I made another trip to Malvern, accompanied this time by my son James, whose health was also in a feeble condition; we remained at Gully's establishment for several weeks, and both derived much benefit from it.

We then travelled over a large portion of England, Ireland, and Scotland, visiting the principal cathedrals and works of art on our way, as well as the Lakes in England and the Giant's Causeway in Ireland.

We afterwards crossed over to Paris, where we remained for several weeks visiting those curiosities and works of art to which strangers are usually attracted. The present Emperor was at that time elected President of the Republic, and we witnessed on several occasions the noise and confusion that were of daily occurrence at that time in the National Assembly.

We returned in November to New Orleans by way of

the West Indies. I again commenced business; but after a few months' practice my head and eyes gave me so much uneasiness that the doctors advised me to withdraw from [business and to travel about for health and amusement.

I therefore arranged my affairs, by taking into co-partnership for that purpose my former bookkeeper, Mr. Turpin, to settle up all the outstanding business; and in 1849, accompan ed by my son, made a tour of the Northern States and Canada.

On our passage up the St. Lawrence in a steamer from Quebec, there were on board a large number of immigrants from the north of Ireland, who had landed the previous day from an emigrant ship and were on their way towards the west. About fifty of those poor people laid themselves down near the engine upon the lower deck, and there met with a dreadful accident. The engineer having lain down to sleep left the engine in charge of a raw assistant, who, not thoroughly under-standing the machinery, opened a valve which let on the whole force of the steam, by which the head of the condenser was blown off, and the poor immigrants were instantly enveloped in a dense cloud of high-pressure steam, by which all were more or less scalded, and thirty of them so badly injured as to die during the night or the next morning.

We never witnessed such suffering and distress, nor passed such a miserable night as on that occasion. There were no medicines nor appliances of any kind on board by which their sufferings could be miti-gated ; the only thing to be found was some wheat-flour, and with this, as far as it went, we dusted over their scalded surfaces. Could we have procured some cotton-wool with which to cover them, their agony might have been diminished, but there was none on board. James and I, and the other first-class passengers, being on the upper deck, escaped uninjured.

We then passed on to the Falls of Niagara, and remained there a week enchanted and bewildered by the sight and sound of that sublime spectacle.

We went on to Saratoga, and, after passing a couple of weeks at that resort of fashion and dissipation, removed to Newport, Rhode Island, where we remained at the Ocean House for nearly a month, and then returned to New York, whence we took a passage for New Orleans by the steamship *Ohio*. On our voyage we had reached somewhere near Cape Hatteras, when the steamer happened to strike upon a reef of rocks that had not been laid down upon the charts; she got off again, however, without other damage than stripping a portion of the copper from her keel. Some two hundred second-class passengers from New England were on board going out to California, and a more noisy and unruly set of men it was never my fate to encounter. They constantly came upon the quarter-deck and took possession of the seats, and spit about their tobacco to the disgust and annoyance of the ladies. As soon as the steamer struck, one of those men got upon the capstan and addressed the crowd on the forward-deck. He said, " As there are but four boats on board, in case of danger of course not half the passengers can be taken in them; I therefore propose, if we see it necessary, that we take possession of the boats, make the best of our way towards the land, and let the first-class nobs and their ladies shift for themselves. " This proposal was hailed with a cheer, and as each of them was armed with a revolver or bowie-knife, they would be ugly customers to contend with; but as the steamer backed off from the reef without injury there was happily no occasion for putting their magnanimity to the test.

Shortly after reaching New Orleans I determined upon retiring finally from business, and having settled up my affairs I caused a copartnership to be entered into between my son James, John Turpin, and Richard Esterbrook, to carry on the business upon their own account. I rented to them my building establishment, with the use of my library and fixtures; and as each of the partners had a separate department to manage, James having the architectural, Turpin the book-keeping and financial, and Esterbrook the mechanical department, they went on very successfully for several years.

In the spring of 1850 it was my good fortune to be introduced to a lady, Miss Catharine Robinson, of the city of Mobile, whose genius, acquirements, and personal advantages made upon me so lasting an impression, that after a short acquaintance I proposed marriage, was accepted, and in the month of July, at the city of Charleston, I had the happiness of making her my wife. We then went to New York and took a passage for Liverpool, where we safely arrived and passed on to London. After having had the pleasure of showing my wife the chief curiosities to be seen in London and Paris, we returned again to New York in the autumn, and passed some weeks very pleasantly among the relations of my wife in the state of Massachusetts.

We then set out for the south by the western route, visiting on our way the Falls of Niagara and the Mammoth Cave of Kentucky, which I consider two of the greatest wonders of nature. We then passed down the rivers Ohio and Mississippi to the city of New Orleans, where we put up at the St. Charles Hotel. A few weeks afterwards that noble building had the misfortune to be burnt to the ground. It had been finished and occupied in 1837, and the principal lessee had already realised a fortune. He had left before the fire took place. The hotel has since been rebuilt upon the old foundations and agreeably to the original plans, with some slight deviations, the chief of which was dispensing with the dome, which, though very beautiful, was costly, and added but little to the value of the building as an hotel.

In January, 1851, my wife and I took passage in a steamer from New Orleans to Havana, where we safely arrived and remained until April, when we returned to New York. We then, in company with the Hon. J. M. Niles, went to Europe and made an extensive tour over Scotland, England, France, Switzerland, and Italy, reaching Naples in November, where my wife gave birth to a daughter. Shortly after that event we returned to the city of Rome, and after two months' stay in the Eternal City we visited Florence, where Mr. Niles parted from us to return homeward. In the month of April, 1852, we had the misfortune to lose our dear little Nina at Florence, by whooping cough, which was at that time very fatal among the children of that city. After that grievous loss we visited Venice, where we remained some weeks enjoying the charms of its delicious climate and admiring the beauties of its palaces, its gondolas, and the various attractions peculiar to that "Queen of the Adriatic."

From Venice we returned by short stages to Milan, and were there charmed by the grandeur and beauties of its splendid cathedral.

We passed on to the Lake Como, where we fell in with friends whom we had known at Naples, and along with them crossed the Alps into Switzerland, remaining some months at the Hotel Byron on Lake-Geneva.

We afterwards returned to Paris, and thence to London; and, after a short stay in England, sailed from Liverpool for Philadelphia.

I made inquiries and some efforts to procure a pleasantly-situated property in the vicinity of Philadelphia, with the intention of making it our future place of residence; but not succeeding in this I tried Baltimore and its neighbourhood, but with only a similar want of success : the truth is, we had become too fastidious in the choice of a location, from the many beautiful spots we had seen in our wanderings over Europe. So we returned to Hartford in Connecticut, and decided upon passing the following winter there at the house of our friend Mr. Niles.

At that time I received a pressing invitation from my son to visit him at New Orleans, as he was about to take unto himself a wife : so, leaving my wife at Hartford, I set out by sea from New York and in due time arrived safely at New Orleans.

Before leaving New York, I for the first time heard of Andrew Jackson Davis, the clairvoyant, and of his writings on spiritualism. I provided myself with copies of the books published by him and others on the subject up to that time, and I read them on the voyage with so much interest and serious reflection that I determined to inquire more fully about the then novel theory of spiritualism as soon as an opportunity should offer.

At New Orleans I saw the lady whom my son intended

to make his wife; she was the daughter of a worthy and respected creole, whom I had known for many years; she was young, handsome, and amiable; so I of course accorded my hearty approval of his choice.

After a short stay at New Orleans, I took a passage on board the steamer " *Crescent City* " for New York, and all went well on the voyage until we had arrived at about the latitude of Charleston; we then encountered an accident which had nearly proved fatal to the steamer and to all on board. We were running in the night against a strong north wind, when at 2 a.m. our captain chanced to go up on deck and saw a large ship in full sail bearing down upon us before the wind; the captain, horrified at the sight, called out to our steersman to put the helm hard down; this was done, and our steamer's head turned a little to one side; but he saw there was not time to clear the ship in that way, so he called again to reverse the helm, and by this means our steamer's head moved towards the ship, our stern moving in the opposite direction; so that by this manœuvre the ship just passed clear of us, with no other damage to our steamer than that of crushing the boat which hung at her quarter, and tearing away the irons by which it was suspended. Had our captain been but a few seconds later in going on deck our steamer would have been struck upon the quarter, and would have inevitably been sent to the bottom with all on board, as the passengers were all in bed at the moment; but, as " a miss is as good as a mile, " we fortunately escaped unhurt.

I arrived at Hartford without further accident, and passed the winter there very pleasantly, until the month of May, 1854, when my wife and I set out again for Europe, and after a short stay in Paris went into Switzerland; passed the summer at various points about the Lake of Geneva and along the Rhine. We returned to Paris in the autumn, and took apartments in the Avenue des Champs-Elysées, where we remained until the following spring. I was much interested during the winter in watching the progress of the building for the Grand Exposition, as it approached towards a finish; and much more so, when that splendid display of the arts and manufactures of all nations was opened to the public that were brought together for the improvement of the people. It was just opposite our house where an Italian assassin made an attempt to shoot the Emperor. I heard the report of the two pistol shots that were aimed at him, and I ran out among the crowd that instantly collected on the spot who were about to execute summary vengeance upon the wretched Italian. The Emperor, who was on horseback, coolly called out to leave the man uninjured and to hand him over to the police. This was instantly done, and the Emperor apparently unmoved rode off towards the Bois de Boulogne, where he met the Empress, and returned with her in an open carriage towards Paris surrounded by an immense crowd of people who enthusiastically shouted " Vive l'Empereur! vive l'Impératrice! "

In the summer of 1855, we visited the springs of Hombourg for several weeks, drinking of their saline waters and enjoying the amusements peculiar to that centre of gambling and dissipation, without, however, joining in the play.

I then considered it necessary that I should return to New Orleans and look after the condition of my property there; and, as my wife by that time had become tired of travelling, we agreed that I should visit New Orleans alone, while she would reside with friends of ours who were living at Lake Constance in Switzerland until my return; this being arranged, I went to visit my father in Ireland, then returned to England, and sailed from Southampton for Havana and thence to New Orleans, where I arrived on the first of November, and found my son, his wife and child all well and in comfortable circumstances.

For nearly a year prior to that period I was much harassed by a catarrh and irritable sore throat, but it had by this time become so much worse that I was obliged to confine myself to the house for the greater part of the winter. I was at last so fortunate, however, as to procure the attendance of Doctor Cox, of New Orleans, who had for many years made diseases of that kind a special study; and who by the judicious use of inhaling mixtures brought my malady under such control as to enable me to stay in the open air during mild or warm weather; but when it is cold or damp I am to this day obliged to wear a respirator.

Having passed the winter at New Orleans, I sailed for New York in May, 1856, where I safely arrived and remained for a month. I then embarked for Havre, where I landed and passed forward through Paris, Bâle, and Constance to Kreuzlingen in Switzerland, where I joined my dear wife after an absence of nine months. While staying at that place some friends suggested that from that time I should write a short sketch of the most important places we might happen to visit in our future wanderings; and I commenced with the place at which we were then staying.

Lake Constance, called by the Germans Boden See, was anciently known to the Romans under the name of Lacus Brigantinus: it is bordered by the territories of five different states — Baden, Würtemberg, Bavaria,

Austria, and Switzerland, and a portion of its coasts belongs to each of those states.

St. Gall is the capital of a canton and one of the principal seats of manufacturing industry in Switzerland. The antique walls which surround the town call to mind the ancient history of St. Gall. It was in the early part of the seventh century that St. Gallus, an Irish monk, left his convent in the Island of Iona, one of the Hebrides, and, after travelling over a large part of Europe converting the heathen, finally settled on the banks of the Steinach, then a wilderness. He taught the wild people of the country the arts of agriculture as well as the doctrines of Christianity. The humble cell which the Irish missionary had founded became the nucleus of civilization; and fifty years after his death it was replaced by a more magnificent edifice, founded under the auspices of Pepin d'Heristal. This abbey was one of the oldest ecclesiastical establishments in Germany: it became the asylum of learning during the dark ages, and was the most celebrated school in Europe between the eighth and tenth centuries. Here the works of the Greek and Latin authors were taught and copied by the obscure monks of the abbey of St. Gall, and preserved in manuscript; among them, Quintilian, Silius Italicus, Ammian Marcellinus, and part of Cicero, may be mentioned. The convent library contains some curious MSS. from Ireland, or transcribed by the Irish monks.

Our residence at the lake was close to the ancient city of Constance, which now contains only 7,500 inhabitants, instead of 40,000 which it is said to have once possessed; it is remarkable for its antiquity, as its streets and many of its buildings remain unaltered since the 15th century. The Minster is a handsome Gothic

structure, begun in 1052; the nave is supported by
16 pillars, each in a single block, and dates from the
13th century. The spot where Huss stood, when sen-
tence of death by burning was pronounced upon him by
his unrighteous judges, is still pointed out. Two sides
of the ancient cloisters, whose arches are filled in with
beautiful tracery, are in good preservation.

In a field, outside of the town, where Huss was burnt,
a monument is placed, consisting of a large boulder
stone with a brass plate attached to it, on which is
engraved a short account of the death of Huss. This has
been lately set up on the spot where that barbarous
act was perpetrated.

In 1474 a perpetual treaty of peace was concluded at
Constance between Sigismund of Austria and the Swiss
Confederation, which put an end to the contests which
for more than a century and a half had existed between
them. Constance belonged to Austria from 1549 to
1805, when by the treaty of Presburgh it was transferred
to Baden.

From Constance we passed on to Zurich, which is the
most important manufacturing town of Switzerland,
containing about 15,000 inhabitants. A Roman station, *Turicum*, fixed on this spot, gave rise to the town.
The cathedral, erected in the 10th century, is a heavy
massive building, very plain within and without; its
nave is supported on square pillars and round arches.
Lavater, the author of the renowned work on physiog-
nomy, was born at Zurich. The old arsenal contains
some ancient armour; also a cross-bow said to be that
with which William Tell shot the apple from his son's
head. From Zurich we went to Berne, which owes its
foundation in the 12th century to Berchtold the Fifth,

Duke of Zahringen, who held the office of warden or proprietor of Western Switzerland from the Emperor of
Germany. To raise up a counterpoise to the overbearing
noblesse he collected the scattered peasantry into com-
munities, the chief of which he formed in 1191, on a peninsula, and fortified it by strong walls. Behind these
the craftsman, the merchant, and all others who needed
protection for their person and property here found it.
Berchtold succeeded in having it acknowledged as a free
town of the empire, independent of all sovereigns but
the Emperor. Invited by these advantages, not only
persons of the poorer sort but many of the inferior
nobles settled here to enjoy the proferred freedom;
but these, together with the more flourishing class of
citizens, in a short time engrossed in their own hands
the entire administration of government; their numbers
being limited, and the right of citizenship hereditary,
they soon formed an aristocracy as powerful in proportion to the extent of the state as that of Venice and
Nuremberg, and as proud as any feudal noblesse in
Europe. The great council of the canton was in process
of time filled solely by the higher burghers, and all
elections were renewed from their own body. Thus
public offices were monopolized for ages by certain
families; and of the most ancient families of burghers
only a small number were actually the rulers, so that in
1785 they consisted of only 69 families. Such a state
of things naturally gave rise to great discontent among
the lower class of citizens; not so much from any public
abuses of their rulers, as from their overbearing haugh-
tiness, and the secresy with which all their proceedings
were conducted. By the French Revolution this ancient
aristocracy lost much of its power; and the events
which followed that of July, 1830, have stripped it of the

remainder. A new constitution, passed and approved by an assemblage of the inhabitants of the canton, now gives to every citizen equal political rights.

We then visited Lausanne, which is the capital of the canton de Vaud, and contains about 15,000 inhabitants. The Pays de Vaud was originally subject to the dukes of Savoy, but, having been conquered by the Bernese, remained tributary to that republic for 250 years, until 1798, when it purchased its own independence. The cathedral is an extensive building, and internally the finest Gothic church in Switzerland; it was founded A. D. 1000, and some traces of the original edifice may be noticed in the groined arches behind the altar; with this exception the building dates from 1275. The interior is very beautiful and singular in its construction.

Among the monuments within the church are a mailed effigy of Otho of Gransom, and the tomb of Victor Amadeus VIII, who was duke of Savoy, bishop of Geneva, and pope under the title of Felix V. Here is also interred the venerated Bernard de Menthon, founder of the Hospice of the Great St. Bernard, which is named after him. Lausanne possesses a college founded in 1587. At this place the historian Gibbon completed his history of Rome. From Lausanne we went on to the city of Geneva, which though the capital of the smallest of Swiss cantons, except Zug, is the most populous town in the Confederation, since it contains 30,000 inhabitants. It is divided into the upper and lower town; and this distinction, arising from the uneven nature of the ground, is perpetuated in the rank and condition of the inhabitants of the two divisions. The upper town consists of the handsome dwellings of the burgher aristocracy, while the lower town is the seat of trade. Although Geneva is a great focus of attraction

to travellers of all nations, it is not as a town very pre-
possessing ; it has but few fine buildings, and very few
sights.

On an island in the middle of the Rhone traces may,
it is said, be discovered of a Roman structure, supposed
to be the foundations of one of the towers erected by
Julius Cæsar to prevent the Helvetians from crossing
the river. The earliest mention of Geneva occurs in
his Commentaries, where it is described as " the last
fortress of the Allobroges, and nearest to the Helvetian
frontier." At this place was born Jean-Jacques Rous-
seau, son of a watchmaker. The staple manufacture of
Geneva from which it derives its chief commercial prosperity is that of watches and jewellery. The first watch
brought to Geneva was in 1587, and at the present time
upwards of 100,000 are manufactured annually. A
committee of master workmen, with a syndic at their
head, are appointed to inspect every workshop and the
articles made in it, to prevent fraud in the quality of
the metals employed in a branch of industry of so great
an advantage to Geneva.

On leaving Geneva we visited Besançon, which
stands on the line of navigation formed to connect the
Rhine with the Rhone; it was the ancient Vesontio, mentioned by Cæsar, in the vicinity of which he defeated
Ariovistus. There are still remains of the ancient city,
consisting of pillars, and other fragments, mosaics,
inscriptions, etc.; there is also a triumphal arch still
tolerably perfect. The Porte Taillée, on the east side, is
an ancient gateway, built in a cleft of the rock which
was tunnelled through by the Romans for the passage of an aqueduct constructed by them to convey
water to the city from the village of Arcier, seven miles
distant.

From Besançon we went forward to the city of Lyons, which claims to have been founded by Greeks 590 years before Christ. It was certainly an important Roman city, and was called Lugdunum, founded by Munatius Plancus (B. C. 40). Here Augustus and Severus resided. The central fountain in the Jardin des Plantes stands in the arena of a Roman Amphitheatre. Here still exist traces of the vast aqueduct constructed, it is said, by the soldiers of Marc Antony, when his legions were quartered at this place, to supply the town with water from the distant mountains of La Forez.

Remains of Agrippa's four great roads, which, radiating from Lyons to the Pyrénées, through the Cevennes to the Rhine, to Marseilles and to the Ocean through Picardy, may still be traced. During the 12th and part of 13th centuries Lyons was held and governed by its archbishops, who obtained a grant of it from the Emperor of Germany; but it was restored to the French crown in the reign of Philippe-le-Bel.

The silk manufacture was established here in the middle of the 15th century by Italian refugees, but it was nearly ruined by the revocation of the Edict of Nantes, which dispersed most of its best workmen to Spitalfields, Amsterdam, Crefeld, etc.

The Roman Catholics and the Protestants, in the 16th century, alternately committed atrocities in the town, which could only be exceeded by those of 1793.

Lyons stands on both banks of the Saône and Rhône, but the largest part occupies the tongue of land between these two rivers; the suburb of La Croix, which is the chief place of the silk weavers, is here situated.

On leaving Lyons we visited Avignon, the ancient city of the Popes, which though now numbering only

32,000 inhabitants, possessed down to the time of Louis the 14th 80,000.

The popes gained possession of Avignon by a grant made by Joanna of Naples; she was to receive for it 80,000 gold crowns, but they were never paid. The popes who reigned at Avignon, beginning with Clement the Fifth, 1305, and ending with Gregory the Eleventh, 1370, numbered seven in all. Afterwards, there were three schismatic popes residing here, from 1378 to 1424.

On the termination of the schism, Avignon became the residence of the papal legate to Louis the 14th, "the eldest son of the Church," who then seized Avignon to revenge an affront on his ambassador at Rome. Louis the 15th held possession of it for ten years, but it was not united with France until 1791. The ancient palace of the popes is an edifice founded by Clement the 5th in 1319; during the greater part of the 14th century, it was the seat of the papal court. Petrarch was here a guest; Giotto and his scholars adorned its walls, and in its dungeons Rienzi was a prisoner. These old battlemented walls and towers defied for several years a French army under Marshal Bouçicault, who besieged within them the anti-pope Benedict the 13th.

From Avignon we went onward to Nismes, where I was deeply interested in the Roman monuments of that ancient city. The Amphitheatre les Arênes, oval on the plan, consists of two stories, each having 60 arcades 70 feet high; the arches in the upper arcade are double, but the inner arches are not concentric with those outside. It is in much better preservation than the Coliseum at Rome, although it was used as a fortress during the middle ages; and retains even its projecting stones above the cornice, pierced with holes for inserting the poles to which the awnings used for covering over the arena were attached.   There were originally 32 rows of seats, of which some of them still remain ; and it is calculated that the number of spectators the building could accommodate was between 18,000 and 20,000. The dimensions of the building are, length 437 feet, width 332 feet, height 70 feet.

The Maison carrée, the name given to a beautiful Corinthian temple, which is still in a state of fine preservation, was a temple consecrated in the reign of Augustus ; it became afterwards a Christian church, and, in the 11th century, the Hôtel de Ville.   At various dates since then it has been used for various purposes, and finally is at present converted into a museum, containing such ancient architectural ornaments and sculptures as have been found about the town and its vicinity.

The Pont du Gard is one of the grandest monuments the Romans left in France ; like Stonehenge, it is the monument of a people's greatness.   It consists of three tiers of arches ; the lowest of six arches, supporting eleven of equal span in the central tier , surmounted by thirty-five of smaller size ; the whole is in a simple style of architecture destitute of ornament.   It is by its magnitude and the skilful fitting of its enormous blocks that it makes so great an impression upon the mind. After the lapse of sixteen centuries, the colossal monument still spans the valley, joining hill to hill, in a nearly perfect state, only the upper part of the northern extremity being broken away. The highest range of arches carries a covered canal about five feet high and two feet wide ; its use was to convey to the town of Nismes the water from two springs twenty-five miles distant.   The arches of the middle tier are formed of three distinct ribs or bands, apparently unconnected.   The height of the Pont du Gard is 180 feet, and the length of the highest arcade 873 feet. The work is attributed to M. Agrippa, son-in-law of Augustus (B. C. 19.).

From Nismes we visited Vichy, which is situated in the valley of the Allier; it is one of the most frequented watering places in France, and is daily increasing in reputation. The Emperor Napoleon III has gone there every season for the past few years. The mineral springs are for the most part alkaline. The waters have been compared to heated soda water, their principal ingredients being carbonate of soda and carbonic acid gas in excess; this acid is combined with soda, potash, and lime; but the most important ingredient is the bicarbonate of soda resulting from this combination. There are eight principal springs, varying in temperature from 56° to 113° Fahren.

Name of spring.	Temperature. Degrees.	Grs. of bicarb. soda in one English pint.
Grande Grille	89.5	44
Puits Chomel..........	104	45
Puits Carré............	113	45
L'Hopital.........	113	45
Lucas....	82.5	45
Lardy.................	77	39
Brosson..............	71.5	44
Celestins............. ...	56	50

There are two bathing establishments, the old and the new, each containing 200 baths. The water is received in stone basins; the baths are very well managed and appointed. The waters have of late years acquired a well-merited celebrity, and have become more and more the rendezvous of English visitors. They are considered to be particularly efficacious in chronic complaints of the liver and digestive organs arising from acidity and from atony; but it is principally in enlargements of the liver, produced by long residence in warm climates, and in hepatic obstructions that they are useful. The same may be said as regards obstructions of the spleen, in diseases of the kidneys and urinary organs, in gout and the glandular affections produced by it. Vichy possesses a large military hospital, whither soldiers are sent from every part of France.

From Vichy we went to Orleans, which was the ancient Roman Genabum, named afterwards Aurelianum, from M. Aurelius, who rebuilt it in the 2d century. It contains 48,000 inhabitants. This was a scene of the chief exploits of Jeanne d'Arc, the Maid of Orléans ; she entered the city on the 20th of April, 1429, in the teeth of the English army, which was vastly superior to the French force. She had convoyed a supply of provisions from Blois to the famished townsmen, who, as she rode in triumph through their streets on her charger in full armour bearing her sacred banner, looked on her as their guardian angel sent from heaven.

We then passed on to Tours, which was a city of some importance in ancient times. The Turones, its ancient inhabitants, joined the league of the sixty-three Gallic towns under Vercingetorix against Julius Cœsar, and are mentioned by Lucan. Touraine was bestowed as an *apanage* on Mary, Queen of Scots, and her husband Francis. At the prefecture is placed the public library of 40,000 volumes, including some curious manuscripts : for example, a copy of the Gospels in gold letters on vellum of the 8th century, which belonged to the church of Saint Martin, upon which the King of France took the oaths as premier chanoine of that church. The present town, the chief of the department Indre-et-Loire, contains 35,000 inhabitants. The principal building is the cathedral of Saint-Gratien, which dates from about 1510. The two towers which flank it are 205 feet high. The interior is 256

feet long and 85 feet high. The choir was begun in
1170, and the nave carried on to completion in the reign
of Saint Louis, but the west end is of the 15th century.
A circular and machicolated tower, the only remaining
part of the castle built by Henry 2d of England in the
12th century, is at present inclosed within the cavalry
barracks. Two towers, one called the Tour de Saint
Martin, the other La Tour de Charlemagne, deserve no-
tice as being the only remaining relics of the Cathedral
of Saint Martin of Tours. The palladium of this building was the shrine of Saint Martin, the first metropoli-
tan of Tours (A.D. 340), which was to the people of that
age what Delphi was to the Greeks—the oracle which
kings and chiefs came to consult in the seventh century.
The concourse of pilgrims to this shrine occasioned the
old Roman town Cœsarodunum to swell to ten times
its original extent. This great ecclesiastical establishment spread civilisation and religion through the country,
and its archbishop became the patriarch of France and
one of the most influential persons in the state. At the
head of the chapter even the kings of France were proud
to enrol themselves. After flourishing for twelve centuries the church was utterly destroyed at the revolution,
excepting two towers out of the five which adorned it.
Tours was long famed for its manufacture of silk, established in 1480 by Louis 11th, who brought over and
settled here Italian weavers ; but this trade from various
causes dwindled away at Tours to take root at Lyons.

From Tours we visited the Celtic monuments of Carnac.
The principal monument is the most extensive of
its kind in France, and is situated about three-quarters
of a mile from the remote village of Carnac, not far
from Nantes. The wild heath on which these stones
were once placed has now become nearly all cultivated.

A few years ago there stood on the dreary heath rude blocks of granite set on end, angular, and moss covered, showing the great length of time they must have stood in that position. The great mass of the stones were arranged in eleven lines, forming ten avenues, with a curved row of eighteen stones at one end, touching at its extremities the two outside rows. There were, it is said, not less than 12,000 stones, being blocks of the granite which forms the basis of the country, and which is barely covered with soil, and in many places projects naked above it. None of the blocks exceed 18 feet in height, and a very large number are cubical masses not more than three feet high. Of the numerous theories invented by antiquaries to account for the origin and object of these stones, it is supposed that it was a burial place on the site of a great battlefield, and that each stone marked a grave. It was probably connected with some of those rights of initiation which formed part of the Druidical religion, and were derived from the same source as the Greek mysteries.

At about three-quarters of a mile north-west of the village of *Locmariaker* (*i. e.* place of the Virgin Mary), there is a mound called *butte de Cæsar*, and near to it is *Dol ar marchant*, the merchant's table, consisting of two table stones, one of them 16 feet by 12, supported on three vertical ones; it is possible to creep under it, and remark the singular figures cut on its under surface.

Locmariaker is supposed to occupy the site of the ancient Dariorigum, the capital of the Venetes. The peninsula of Rhuys contains the following objects of curiosity. First, Le Grand Mont, situated about four miles from Sarzeau, an obscure little town, but memorable as the birthplace of the author of Gil Blas. It is the largest tumulus existing in France, 100 feet high and 300 feet in circumference.

From Carnac we went forward to Poitiers, which, historically, is a very celebrated city. The invading tide of the Saracenic hordes penetrated in the 8th century thus far into western Europe, at a time when the fate of Christianity seemed trembling in the scale. At that epoch, having already conquered Spain, they poured through the defiles of the Pyrenees, overspread Aquitaine, advanced up to the walls of Poitiers, under their famed chief Abdelrahmen, and burned the church of Saint Hilaire to the ground. They were even threatening to pass the Loire, when they were met between Poitiers and Tours by Charles Martel, in 732. This contest between the Gospel and the Koran ended in the defeat of the Saracens, 300,000 of whom, it was said, were left dead on the field, and the remnant retired never more to trouble Christendom in the west.

At an earlier period, in 507, the plains of Poitiers had been the scene of the defeat of Alaric, King of the Visigoths, by Clovis.

Poitiers is celebrated in Engl'sh history by the victory gained under its walls by the Black Prince over King John of France, who was thence led into captivity.

From Poitiers we passed on to Bordeaux, which is the second seaport town of France, and contains 124,000 inhabitants. One of its most conspicuous and handsomest buildings is the theatre, which is of good Italian architecture of the Corinthian order. It is isolated on all sides, and is situated in the very centre of the town: it was erected in 1780, under the direction of the architect Louis.

Near the east end of the cathedral, but quite detached

from it, is the Tour de Peyberland, a noble structure 200 feet high, square below, and supported by buttresses, but gradually diminishing from its base until it terminates in a circular top. It was originally surmounted by a spire, which rose to a height of 300 feet. It is named from Pierre Berland, who rose from being the son of a poor labourer in Medoc to be Bishop of Bordeaux; he caused it to be erected in 1430. Bordeaux still retains a monument of the Roman city *Burdigala*, in the fragment of an amphitheatre, now called Palais Gallien, but though possibly built in the reign of the Emperor Gallienus, it was not a palace, but a circus, capable of containing 1,500 persons.

The earliest mention of Bordeaux is by Strabo. Hadrian created it the capital of 2d Aquitania. It belonged for nearly 300 years to the kings of England, who obtained it by the marriage of Eleanor of Guienne with Henry 2d in 1152. Here Henry, son of the Black Prince, was born.

From Bordeaux we went to Toulouse, which is situated in the midst of the great plain of Gascony and Languedoc: it was the ancient capital of Languedoc, and numbers at present 78,000 inhabitants. It is interesting from its historical souvenirs, as the capital of the kingdom of the Visigoths, from 413 to 507, when it was destroyed by Clovis. But the most tangible relics of its former days were destroyed at the time of the Revolution. L'Église Saint Sernin, the oldest, largest, and most perfect ecclesiastical edifice of the town, is built of brick and stone in the Romanesque style: it was finished and consecrated in 1090 by Pope Urban 2d. It is a curious monument of antiquity, and conspicuous for its lofty octagonal tower, formed by five tiers of arches, each storey less in size than that below it. The Museum boasts of possessing the ivory horn of the renowned Roland richly carved. Here, on the 10th of April, 1814, was fought the great battle between the French and the Allies, under Soult and Wellington; the Allies had 52,000 men and the French 38,000, according to Colonel Napier. The Allies lost in the battle 4,659 men and four generals; the French nearly 3,000 and five generals killed or wounded.

We then went forward to Narbonne, which is a city of 1,200 inhabitants, and though once important, it is now not even the *chef-lieu* of the department. It was the *Narbo Martius* of the Romans, one of the first colonies established by them beyond the Alps, and capital of the vast province of Gallia Narbonensis, which extended from the Alps to the Pyrénées. It was the spot where Julius Cæsar settled the remains of his tenth legion, at the termination of the civil wars; yet it retains very scanty vestiges of its ancient masters, compared with the celebrity it maintains in history. Not one Roman building is now left, all the remains and traces of its former splendour were built into the town walls which were erected under Francis the First.

From Narbonne we passed forward to Marseilles, and remained in its vicinity for a month. The port or old harbour of Marseilles is a natural basin 1,000 yards long by 330 broad, extending into the heart of the town, covering an area of nearly 70 acres, and is capable of receiving more than 2,000 vessels at a time; it has most of the disagreeable features of an ordinary seaport, and some very offensive ones which are peculiarly its own; but extensive improvements are now going on which will soon remove those objections. This is the focus of that extensive commerce which renders Marseilles the most important seaport of the Mediterranean; it dates back nearly 3,000 years, from the time when the Phocæans first landed on her shore, introducing among the barbarous people of western Europe the civilization of the East.

The Museum contains the few relics of antiquity which alone remain of the ancient city of Massilia, founded (B. C. 578) by the Phocæan exiles flying from Asia Minor. None of the antiquities now remaining are so old as the capture of the city by Julius Cæsar.

Leaving Marseilles by steamer we arrived at Genoa, called " La Superba," which is a free port where goods may be warehoused and re-exported free of duty. It is the chief outlet on the Mediterranean for the manufactures of Switzerland, Lombardy and Piedmont; and Lombardy receives many of its imported foreign articles through it. The harbour is protected by two moles, the opening between the two heads of which is 595 yards. The resident population of the town is about 110,000. The manufacture of silks, velvets, and damasks employ many of the inhabitants. The Genoese are laborious, robust and well looking. Their dialect is very peculiar, nearly unintelligible to strangers.

The fortifications were in the first instance erected to protect the city against the Sardinian army under the Duke of Savoy, and they were in a great measure raised by voluntary contributions. Upwards of 10,000 men worked upon them without receiving either pay or provisions. One Carmelite friar raised 100,000 lire by collections at his sermons.

The streets of Genoa are generally very narrow, and the palaces and houses very high. The palaces are especially remarkable for the richness of their architecture and the splendid collections of works of art which they contain. The Duomo, or Cathedral of St. Lorenzo, was

built in the 11th century, and restored about 1300.   In
some parts of the edifice are inscriptions from which it
is ascertained that the north side was completed in 1307,
and the south side in 1312.   It is related by one inscription that the city was founded by Janus 1st, King of
Italy, the grandson of Noah; and how Janus 2d, Prince
of Troy, took possession of the city founded by his an-
cestor.   These inscriptions are engraved in capital letters exactly in the form employed in coeval manuscripts,
and are fine specimens of lapidary caligraphy.   The
richest portion of this church is the Chapel of St. John
the Baptist, into which no female is permitted to enter
except on one day of the year, an exclusion imposed by
Pope Innocent the 8th.   The screen which divides it
from the chuch is of rich *cinquecento* Gothic, and was
completed about the year 1496.   The city now presents
an aspect of faded grandeur; its beautiful palaces are too
large and their decorations too rich for the fortunes of
their present occupants.

Leaving Genoa we passed on by way of Leghorn to
Florence, and there hired apartments for the winter.
Florence has been called ''the beautiful,'' but this description is somewhat exaggerated.   The river Arno un-
equally divides the city, three quarters being on the north,
and one on the south side.   The river is sometimes a
shallow stream, then a furious torrent, but at all times
muddy and discoloured.   Three spacious bridges span
the river ; two are of modern and elegant construction,
and the third, Ponte Vecchio, is very ancient, with
shops and stalls upon it, as in the olden time.   The
houses along the streets are lofty, but have a gloomy
appearance.   The galleries of paintings and statuary
are the great attractions of Florence;   and, among
strangers, the business of life appears to be looking at

works of art and talking about them. It has been very properly said that architecture, sculpture, and painting ought to be discriminated : the first cannot be considered as an imitative art, while sculpture and painting are strictly so, the marble and the canvas alike appealing to the memory as to the fancy.

The Sagrestia affords a fine specimen of Michael Angelo's skill as a sculptor, while the building itself displays equally his architectural taste. What a gigantic intellect was his : painting, sculpture, architecture, fortification, theology, and poetry, employed by turns his universal genius. It appears reasonable to conclude that it was not in the academy, so much as in the workshops, that the Tuscan artists contrived to develope their genius. It was the use of pictures, which, among them, gave nutrition to art. Raffaelle died at Rome in 1520; Michael Angelo outlived him more than forty years. A short time before that period, the Italians having manifested a tendency towards searching investigations in science, the Church marked out a line which science was not permitted to overstep, while poetry and art were encouraged in every possible way ; the works of the artists became, therefore, chiefly of a religious character ; Ludovico Caracci laboured to embody the ideal of Christ, and produced representations which became models to succeeding painters.

For the deterioration of modern sculpture, one great cause has not been sufficiently considered : this was the separation of sculpture from architecture. The effect of this separation may be comprehended if we examine the Pantheon at Rome, and read the descriptions of it as it stood in the time of Agrippa. The interior was then adorned by the statues of famous men, while a principal object of the building was to contain those memorials in a place worthy of their reception : the niches of the Pantheon still remain, but the statues are gone, and the venerable pile, although still majestic, seems bare and stripped of more than half its beauty.

I visited at various times the studio of my esteemed friend H. Powers, the sculptor, admiring his mechanical skill equally with his artistic genius; the various contrivances for expediting the progress of his works were excellent.

In the course of that winter at Florence I was frequently afflicted by a painful disease by which I was confined to my room for weeks together, so that as soon as the warm sun of summer began to shine we removed to Leghorn, where I was interested in watching the progress of a new mole that was being at that time under construction to protect the entrance to the harbour; the work was formed by blocks of artificial stone composed of puzzolano, clean sand, powdered lime, and quick lime, in equal quantities, ground up together in a mill with water to produce a very soft mortar, which being mixed with a double measure of broken stone produced a strong concrete, which being cast into wooden moulds, filled up in the centre with large lumps of coarse rock, produced blocks 10 feet long, 7 feet wide, and 5 feet high, which required to be kept in the moulds about twenty days before the sides of the moulds could be removed; the blocks were then left exposed to the air for a space of five or six months before they were considered sufficiently hard to be placed in the work. This was at last accomplished by carrying them out upon lighters, towed by a steamer to the works, and lowered into their places by powerful cranes. On leaving Leghorn we landed at Civita Vec-

chia, and from that place went to see the Etruscan
Necropolis, near the modern town of Corneto.

Here are scooped out of the rock tombs which have
endured 3,000 years with slight injury. Excavations
have been made from time to time, and, in recent years,
2,000 tombs have been opened; but it is supposed that
there could not have been less than two millions, as the
Necropolis extended over sixteen square miles. The
principal tombs are shown to travellers. You descend
by a steep short path into what looks like a pit; at the
end of this abrupt descent is a door, which being
unlocked at once introduces you into the sepulchre, a
chamber carved in the rock, dry, clean, and enduring.
Above, on the roof, around the walls, you see figures of
men, animals, etc. The games, funeral processions, ban-
quets, amusements and customs of the Etruscans are
here disclosed. The first we entered was called *Grotto
della Querciola*, the largest of the tombs, but the colours
are faded. The paintings represent horsemen, boar-
hunts, games, groups of dancers, etc. The second
tomb was the *Grotto del Triclinio*, a fine chamber with a
vaulted roof, the paintings representing figures reclining
at a funeral banquet: one of the ladies is in the act of
breaking an egg, and one of the gentlemen is receiving
a cup of wine; a tame leopard, a partridge, and a cock
are picking up the crumbs. On another side is represented a dance, where the castanets are played. The
third tomb was the *Camera del Morto*. This is small, but
highly interesting. One painting exhibits two youthful
figures laying out the dead body of an old man; it might
be supposed to denote two children performing the last
sad duties to a loved parent: a very simple, but touching
representation. Another represents the funeral dances
and ceremonies. The next inspected was the *Grotto del*

Barone, chiefly remarkable for some very spirited sketches of horses in various attitudes. Then comes the *Grotto delle Inscrizione*, of great size and most interesting. Over the door are two tigers; on one side, two figures are standing with a fish, which they hold over a gridiron; on the other, two persons seated at a table are playing with dice. The walls are covered with the greatest variety of groups; wrestlers, boxers, dancers, horsemen, lions, stags, dogs, etc., and various human figures, each having an inscription, which, though legible, cannot be understood or deciphered. This tomb faces the desolate site of the ancient city, the seat of art and power, the once splendid home of those whose features we had but just seen delineated, and whose names we in vain attempted to decipher.

The grotto is very spacious; its roof supported by a square pillar, on which is painted the Angel of Death. Several sarcophagi are here placed on ledges, three of which are on the sides of the wall. There is one very curious painting, though much faded, of a procession of souls, attended by genii to their final abode of happiness. The band is preceded by a good genius, the expression of whose countenance is most pleasing; around his head is twined a serpent, and in his hand he bears a lighted torch. A handsome youth then appears, followed by a monstrous fiend, the hideous embodiment of the evil genius of Etruria; in one hand he carries an instrument resembling a large hammer; the other, terminating in a claw, clutches the shoulders of the youth. A female figure of extreme beauty follows, attended likewise by an evil genius with a serpent round his head. Another highly interesting tomb, the *Grotto del Cardinale*, contains a painting, though fast fading, of a similar character. Two winged genii are dragging in a car to judgment the soul of one deceased : they are each, the one good, the other evil, contending for the exclusive possession of the soul, which the Etruscans seemed to have thought preserved after death the likeness of the body it had quitted, though in a shadowy form.

Such is the present condition of the Necropolis, where two millions of bodies are supposed to have been inter-red of those who were inhabitants of a city older than Rome, and whose race and language have been long extinct.

These people buried their arms and precious orna-ments with the dead, to whom they had belonged in life. Their tombs have been ransacked and laid bare by the raging curiosity of our day, and the ornaments and arms, while they fill the museum of the antiquary, teach us something of the customs and civilization of their owners.

The drawings on the walls of their everlasting tombs inform us the Etruscans believed in a future state of existence; that their warriors and their women, how-ever brave, however beautiful, must by their actions be made happy or the reverse. An Etruscan necropolis must have had a striking effect, crowded with monu-mental mounds, crowned with sphynxes and based upon foundations of solid masonry, with doors all round and having copestones adorned with lions, sphynxes, and griffins; and we perceive how great is the error of those who assert that Etruscan tombs were when constructed buried in the earth. From this place we passed on to Rome.

Although the Roman empire has long passed away, the physical divisions of the ground on which the city stood are still plainly traceable, and how excellent was the site! The Seven Hills were separately places of defence; their summits were healthful, their position commanding. Thus a large tract of land was naturally enclosed as it were for the early Romans; they were not cooped up in a narrow spot or upon a single hill; and they had the Tiber flowing by them to facilitate commerce and give freshness to the city, of which the modern inhabitants do not seem to fully avail themselves. The localities of the Seven Hills may have had a considerable influence in forming the robust character of the Roman people. They profited by their natural advantages, extended their city, guarded it by their valour, and thus became by degrees a renowned and mighty nation. The height of the principal hills above the sea is as follows. The Capitoline, 160 feet; Palatine, 170; Aventine, 118; Cœlian, 116; Esquiline, 180; Quirinal, 150; and the Pincian, 206. The Palatine mount is nearly a mile and a half in circumference and almost square. The Capitoline, containing 16 acres, is about 500 yards long and 185 broad. The Esquiline is the most extensive of the Seven Hills.

Standing on the Piazza in front of St. Peter's Church, one is no less astonished than delighted: it is 729 feet in length, by 606 in breadth. There are two beautiful fountains, one on the right hand, the other on the left, which shoot up water to a considerable height. In the centre, stands the famous Egyptian Obelisk, elevated there under Pope Sixtus; and at either end, in front of the marble steps, stand two majestic statues of St. Peter and St. Paul. Everything we see is stately and imposing except the façade of the church: this is tasteless, and conceals the dome. Over one of the doors in the library of the Vatican may be seen a representation of St. Peter's as Michael Angelo designed it, by which one may see at a glance that according to the plan of the great architect the dome would have been as visible to the eye at once as the dome of St Paul's now is; but at present the cupola is more than half hidden by the facade.

Having crossed the threshold of the stupendous pile, one must pause for some minutes to reverentially contemplate the interior of St. Peter's. People talk and critics write of temporary disappointment on the first view of this vast fabric. I never viewed it with any other feeling than that of mingled surprise, delight, and wonder. Slowly walking along the immense nave, our ideas gradually assume more distinctness, and we are better able to comprehend the whole by an examination of each separate part. Standing under the majestic dome, we behold the realisation of Michael Angelo's boast that he would fling the Pantheon into the air. The high altar with its baldachino is placed under the dome; the twisted columns that support it were made of the bronze stripped from the Pantheon by Urban VIII. A double marble staircase leads down to the confessional or tomb of St. Peter, illuminated by more than a hundred never-dying lamps. The statue of Pius VI., in a kneeling position, is placed before the tomb of the saint : it is one of the finest of Canova's works.

The dome is the next object of unbounded admiration, no less from its design than from its altitude and structure. There is a broad paved way leading to the roof of the church; from thence the dome may be reached by a succession of staircases. The first resting place is the roof of the nave : there can be seen the workshops for mechanics employed in keeping the immense edifice in repair. Then we ascend to the first gallery, where we have the grandest prospect which can be seen in the interior of an earthly building.

The ascent of the second gallery is more steep ; pigmy men may be seen creeping on the pavement below. The fourth stage is into the ball, into which a person can draw himself up by a vertical ladder, but it is not a place from which he can obtain a satisfactory view. The dome we see in the church is not the same we see outside; this latter is only a case or covering to the dome seen within, and it is between the two that the stairs are placed by which we get up into the ball.

Of the various ceremonies witnessed in Rome, none was to me more interesting than the academical exhibition of the pupils belonging to the College of the Propaganda, which was founded for the express purpose of training young men to act as missionaries in other countries; the youths are here taught languages, theology, casuistry, and what ever else may be necessary to fit them for spreading the religion of Rome in remote quarters of the world. The exhibition which I witnessed consisted in delivering short orations and dialogues in fifty one different languages. During the life of the celebrated linguist Cardinal Mezzofanti, he usually presided on these occasions. The training of the youths in the Propaganda is not merely scholastic ; while the mind is tutored, their bodies are strengthened and hardened by vigorous exercises.

Nineteen centuries have rolled away since that celebrated building, the Pantheon, from its symmetry of proportion, was the admiration of ancient Rome, and the marvellous preservation of what still remains justifies the general opinion of its excellence. The portico and dome are exclusively the objects of our external admiration. The portico is but 110 feet long and 40 broad. The pediment and composition of the entablature, combined with the position and arrangement of the columns, give to the whole building an aspect of unrivalled beauty. Raising our eyes to the dome, we see the greatest triumph of original architectural design in the world : Michael Angelo's rapturous praises would alone suffice to prove it to be so. Beneath the dome the bright sky of Italy shines down through a circular aperture in the top. We see the whole building at a glance, are captivated with it, and can scarcely tell why. Its monuments in bas-relief, silver and bronze, are gone. Fifty million pounds weight of metal, it is said, has been torn from it by the Christian spoilers, though spared by the Goths; cathedrals and palaces have been decked out with the plunder ; yet, in naked beauty, the interior still strikes the beholder with delight. The pavement is of the time of Septimus Severus ; it is composed of porphyry and yellow marble, and of pavonazzetto laid down in large slabs alternately round and square. The pavement, piliars, doors, portico and dome are still uninjured.

The way in which the title of Cardinal arose was thus explained by Father Paul, author of the history of the Council of Trent :

‘‘ When churchmen of merit happened by the calamities of war to be driven from their ministry, they fled to Rome and Ravenna, being the richest churches, where they were maintained out of the common purse in the same manner as the clergy of the place. When any vacancy happened, it was filled by some one of the strange clergy, who, being thus provided for, was called *incardinatus*, and he who stepped into a ministry, having had none before, was called *ordinatus.* This usage began in Italy before the year 600, when many bishops and other clergymen were driven from their cures by the ravages of the Lombards, and were thus replaced in other churches as ministries became vacant. The bishops were called *episcopi cardinales*, and the priests *presbyteri cardinales.* Now the greater part of those who were so driven from their own churches, betaking themselves to those of Rome and Ravenna, which had most employment to give, and these strangers finding a welcome reception there, it rarely happened that any of their own people were ordained, and this was the reason why in these two churches all who had any ministry were called *cardinales*, a name which still remains in the Church of Rome, but not in that of Ravenna. Thus the name of *cardinal*, which at first derived itself from a very low and abject condition, is, by change of signification, become a title of elevated dignity."

From Rome we went to Naples, which was originally called Parthenope, from a syren of that name said to have been buried there. The Athenians having planted a colony and built a town, which they called Neapolis, it became a favourite retreat of the luxurious Romans. Rome preserves traces of her glory, but all the proud monuments of grandeur in this region have been swept away. Cities have vanished, lakes dried up, hills have been swallowed by the yawning earth, which again, as in wild sport, has shot forth little mountains from her heaving bosom. Earthquake after earthquake has ravaged this beautiful region, changing all things, even the climate. Poets naturally seized on this wonderful country as the appropriate scene for Tartarus and their Elysium, for here was combined the awful with the beautiful.

It seems strange to moderns that the gay people of

Pompeii should have made a principal entrance to their city by a road lined with the monuments of its dead; but it is remarkable that amidst these tombs stands one of the most interesting houses in Pompeii, the villa of Diomedes, which is built on the slope of a hill, the doorway elevated five or six feet above the street. In the subterranean vaults where wine and oil were stored were found huddled up together the skeletons of seventeen persons covered by a mass of ashes of extreme fineness, supposed to have slowly entered and thus consumed the victims with lingering torments.

The streets are very narrow, with marks of carriage wheels worn into the pavement. The widest of the streets is not 30 feet across. Throughout the streets are signs over the shops that indicated the trades pursued within : for example, two men carrying a vase for wine, served as a sign for a wine-shop; a goat denoted a vendor of milk; and a painting of one boy hoisted upon another's back, undergoing a flagellation, was no doubt a *striking* illustration of the schoolmaster within. The habitations were low and were fronted by a dead wall, which gave them a cheerless aspect not unlike many to be seen in Italy at the present day. Among the buildings was the house of a surgeon, known by the quantity of surgical instruments found therein, most of them made of bronze. A box of pills was discovered, as evidence of the apothecary's art; and a loaf was found with the baker's name stamped upon it. The houses of the tragic poet, of Sallust, of Pansa, of the great and little fountain, are kept locked to preserve the mosaics and frescoes which they contain. The walls of many other houses were covered with drawings of animals. Artists usually make correct copies of them, immediately after the excavation around them is finished.

There are now over one hundred houses uncovered. Where the excavations are actually making there is much bustle among the officials to inspect anything that may turn up. Pompeii was not destroyed by an eruption of lava, but by a suffocating shower of soft fine ashes and cinders, with some liquid matter, which in the course of a week covered the city, penetrating every dwelling and filling up every crevice. The consistence of the matter and its nature accounts for the preservation of the buildings and of their contents. The length of time which it must have required to cover Pompeii with twelve feet of ashes enabled the majority of the inhabitants to escape, though numbers must have perished. The skulls of skeletons were found in the streets which had been fractured by stones projected from Vesuvius five miles distant. Among the public buildings are baths in admirable preservation: they are spacious, and decorated and arranged in excellent taste. The theatres are perfect in form; the seats and stage remain. One theatre, the largest, was without a roof originally, and may have held about 5,000 persons. The small theatre in the same quarter of the city was roofed. The amphitheatre, which is at some distance from the others, would contain 10,000 persons. The public buildings, the temples, theatres, basilica, market, etc., are clustered around the forum. This area, which was covered with slabs of marble, presents the grandest view to be seen in Pompeii. Here are columns, some entire, others broken, some standing, others prostrate, ruined temples and pedestals, and a triumphal arch. There also stand the majestic ruins of the temple of Jupiter; the Basilica or hall of justice, which was 230 feet long and 80 feet broad, sustained by splendid columns, and the Prætor's throne, which are still visible. Here we have an example,

in a provincial town of the empire, of a hall of justice
such as exists not throughout the length and breadth of
the Peninsula in modern times. Justice anciently did
really exist, and was administered with purity and with
external splendour. With respect to the size of Pompeii, its greatest length was not a mile, its area about
160 acres. It was protected by a wall and six gates.
Its situation was close to the seashore, but it is now
half a mile inland. These changes, however great, are
not surprising, considering the nature of the soil and
the revolutions it has undergone.

It is not possible to feel cheerful in Pompeii; whatever
we behold in this strange place reminds us of an awful
catastrophe. We look up to Vesuvius, and the volcano still smokes and occasionally vomits forth its
burning lava, hot stones, and ashes. We know not
whether the fair cities at its base may not be overwhelmed as Herculaneum was by a fiery torrent. Herculaneum presents to the eye but little in comparison with
Pompeii; yet what we do see, because, not extensive, is
more accurately examined and remembered. Descending as if into a square garden, we have before us all
that has been cleared of the lava with which it was enveloped. Even after Pompeii, the remains of the few
houses, with their frescoes and paintings, are deeply
interesting. The theatre, many feet underneath the
town of Portici, is the chief object of attraction. A gallery or subterranean passage has been cut through the
mass of lava which overwhelmed Herculaneum, along
which, by the help of torches, we grope our way till we
reach the orchestra. The seats and form of this vast
theatre are visible. Many valuable statues were here
discovered, and also some admirable pieces of sculpture. Very extensive excavations have been made since

6

1713, when Herculaneum was discovered. The museum of Naples was furnished by these discoveries with a prodigious variety of all the ornamental and useful articles of life, and also with the papyri manuscripts which at the time were considered as invaluable treasures of antiquity. When these treasures were extracted the excavations were again filled up, except those preserving the approach to the benches of the theatre. The mass of matter we actually see covering the city of Herculaneum is a dark grey stone, brittle, and easily cut through; and as it did not adhere to foreign bodies, marbles and bronzes were preserved; it is said that exact models of statues were frequently found in this composition.

Herculaneum may have suffered from the eruption which buried Pompeii, but torrents of lava from subsequent eruptions, which it is now impossible to remove, have covered the unfortunate city to a depth of from 70 to 112 feet. Portici is built over Herculaneum, no doubt in ignorance of its site.

From Naples to the base of the cone of Vesuvius is eight miles. The base of the mountain is covered by the vineyards which produce the pleasant wine called "Lachrymæ Christi."

The ascent at first is gradual; villages, solitary houses, vineyards are passed, and we turn into what may be properly described as a vast field of lava. The ground we now tread was fertile as that behind us; it has been for ever withered, not a green thing is visible, all the works of man and productions of nature have alike been blasted. The colour of the lava, which lies in ugly heaps over the ground through which our path winds, varies in proportion to its age: the older it is, the more earthy is its appearance. The activity of Vesuvius far exceeds that of Ætna. There were great eruptions in 1794, 1805, 1813, 1822, 1831 and 1858. Sometimes lava is poured out from the upper crater of the volcano; at other times the fiery liquid cannot boil up to its mouth, but bursts forth from cavities in the flank of the mountain, and pours into the plain. The lava moves slowly, but with irresistible force. Lava annihilates every particle of vegetable matter it touches, being impregnated with sulphuric and muriatic acid. Having arrived at the base of the cone, a difficulty would arise to individuals who could not undergo the fatigue of ascending, but, by a simple contrivance, this difficulty is surmounted; an arm chair resting on poles, which borne by four stout porters, carries the invalid in safety, though certainly not in ease to the summit.

Deposited on the edge of the first landing, which is about 200 yards in diameter, one feels great heat without perceiving any immediate cause for it. We now walk over an extensive plain of lava, of a black colour, but on thrusting down a stick it yields easily to the pressure, and the red fire will appear through the orifice. Fields of hot lava must be crossed to the inner and upper base of the cone, and in some places the heat is oppressive; little elevations are scattered over this plain from which views of the surrounding country are obtained.

At length we approach the crater, the ascent to which seems as if covered with cinders, brickdust, and rubbish. But what a phenomenon is now before us! Every instant columns of smoke shoot forth, then flame, then volleys of red stones are hurled into the air! The sound which accompanies these eruptions is like thunder underneath the awful mountain. The fiery matter is projected straight up into the air, and along with it, the ignited stones fall back again into the yawning cavern.

It is quite impossible in such a scene to divest the mind
of a sensation of terror; thousands have visited this volcano in safety, yet a sudden destruction might in one
instant overtake us where we presumptuously stand.
The projectile power of this volcano is prodigious; it is
said that large stones have been cast up to a height of
nearly 4,000 feet above the crater, and in the masses of
lava now lying about large pieces of stone are often
involved and hardened.

On the 15th of May, 1858, we took up our residence for
the summer at the hotel Quisisana at Castellamare, and
had from our windows a splendid view of the bay and
city of Naples, with Vesuvius and Pompeii in the distance. On the 30th of May Vesuvius began to throw
out smoke and then lava from several new openings,
round the base of the cone; the eruption after some
days became greater than had occurred for several years
before; when at its greatest, we drove one evening as
close to the cone as it was considered prudent to go,
and found an immense multitude of people collected there
to witness the eruption. The scene presented was the
grandest and the most awful I ever beheld; from the several new openings, situated at points about one-third
the height of the cone from its base, the incandescent
lava was rolling slowly down from each opening towards
the valley; one of these streams, about eighty feet wide
and perhaps from ten to fifteen feet in depth, had already reached a distance of nearly a mile, destroying
every thing in its course, overturning walls and houses,
and filling up hollows where any had existed in its way.
From one of the openings, a mass of lava of about thirty
feet in diameter was ejected to from fifty to a hundred
feet high once in about every ten minutes, and this falling
down again produced a sound like a distant clap of

thunder. The dull red light from the smoking lava, the dense smoke from the openings and the rushing sound of the wind which blew in fiercely from all sides, to supply the place of that rarified air sent up the cone by the heat, produced altogether such a scene as can never be forgotten. After a few days, the eruption of lava began to subside, but smoke continued to issue from the new openings for many months.

In our walks and drives toward Sorento we frequently met the carriages of the King of the Two Sicilies, who always returned our salutations very affably.

On the 8th of September, we saw in Naples a grand procession of the King and all his family at the festa of the Piedigrotta. There were eighteen state carriages, two of which had eight horses to each, the others had six horses to each, attended by a large number of liveried grooms and footmen ; the road along which they passed was lined on each side by all the troops about Naples. No one who then witnessed that grand display could have imagined that in so short a time the family of this King should have lost all dear to them in that beautiful city.

On Sept. 13th, we saw the funeral procession of a general of marine, who, it was said, had attained the age of 105 years. The corpse was dressed in military uniform, and was carried on men's shoulders in an open box or cradle, the body so elevated at the head that the face could be seen by the people in the street.

From Naples we embarked for a visit to Algiers, where after a stormy passage we arrived in safety and remained for several weeks.

Algeria was the ancient kingdom of Numidia ; it was reduced to a Roman province 44 years B. C., but afterwards became independent, until dreading the power of the Spaniards the nation invited Barbarossa the pirate to assist it, and he seized the government A.D. 1516 ; but it afterwards fell to the lot of Turkey. The Algerines for ages braved the resentment of the most powerful states in Christendom, and the Emperor Charles 5th lost a fine fleet and army in an unsuccessful expedition against them in 1541. Algiers was reduced by Admiral Blake in 1653, and terrified into pacific measures with England ; but it repulsed the vigorous attacks of other European powers, particularly those of France in 1688 and 1761, and of Spain in 1775, 1783 and 1784. It was bombarded by the British fleet under Lord Exmouth in 1816, when a new treaty followed, and Christian slavery was then abolished.

Algiers surrendered to a French armament under Bourmont and Duperré, after some severe conflicts, July 5th, 1830, when the Dey was deposed and the barbarian government wholly overthrown. The French ministry announced their intention to retain Algiers permanently on May 20th, 1834. Marshal Clausel defeated the Arabs in two engagements and entered Mascara, December 22nd, 1836. Abd-el-Kader surrendered to General Lamoricière, December 22nd, 1847.

The city of Algiers consists at present of the old town which is built against the side of a steep hill facing the east, the streets so narrow that a person with outstretched arms could almost touch the opposite sides. The modern portion of the city consists chiefly of a principal street running parallel with the sea shore, and on each side of which there are arcades that afford shade and shelter to foot passengers ; but there are such crowds of filthy half-naked Arabs lounging about, that a person is constantly obstructed and annoyed by them ; all the lowest kinds of work are performed by these people, some of whom are strong and active. The Arab and Moorish women in the streets are all veiled to the eyes ; but the Jewish women, who are by far the fairest and most handsome, do not veil the face, but have a peculiar mode of covering and ornamenting the head, leaving the face uncovered.

We drove into the country in various directions. The principal road is that leading to Blida. The country is rough and hilly and the roads are generally bad ; the land where cultivated appears rich in quality, but the culture is rough and slovenly. There are a few farm houses of modern construction, but the bye roads and fences are of the roughest description. I saw some small fields in which cotton had grown ; the plants were tall but few in number. I saw no appearance of vines in the vicinity of Algiers, but I was told they are produced in other parts of the country. Taken as a whole I did not think it a place to which emigrants would be permanently attracted. In the immediate vicinity of the city, there are large plots of ground occupied by Germans in the production of cabbages and other vegetables.

We visited a large mosque in the city, which is arranged and ornamented exactly like what we afterwards saw in Cairo.

A fair was being held outside the town which in all things resembled those fairs usually held at certain seasons of the year at the chief country towns throughout France.

In coming to Algiers it was our intention to pass the winter there, but on examination I found the hotels very costly, and the few private houses were so badly arranged and constructed for warmth, that the cold east winds to which the city is exposed would be insufferable in winter, more especially as the fuel consists chiefly of light faggots such as are used by bakers to heat their ovens. So, finding a trading steamer preparing to go to Malta, touching at the principal places along the coast, I took a passage and went on board on the 17th of October, where we found a party of Americans on their way to the East. On the 18th we entered the bay of Bougie, which is surrounded by immense rocks that spring up abruptly out of the water; the front of the harbour has a number of ancient walls, castles, and other strong places left by the Romans. The present town is built against the hills ranged along the bay, and the hills covered over by brushwood. We had on board several Arab pilgrims on their way to Mecca, one of whom was a chief of some importance among his people; he was among the first-class passengers, and every morning at daylight he perched himself crosslegged upon a shelf in the cabin, and read or chanted aloud portions of the Koran for half an hour.

On the 19th we arrived at Philipville, a modern town built by the French; it has one good street with several shops. We walked to the top of a hill behind the town, where a number of ancient cisterns, cut out of the solid rock by the Romans, are exhibited; but higher up there are other cisterns from which the present town is supplied with water brought from a distant spring through a channel cut in the rock.

On the 20th we landed to visit the town of Stora, but it presented nothing worthy of description.

On the 21st we reached the town of Bône, and went ashore to visit the tomb of Saint Augustine, which stands upon the summit of a hill near the town ; it is a rude structure, in a ruinous condition, with nothing at present interesting in its appearance.

On the 23d of October we entered the gulf of Tunis, which is a long narrow arm of the sea, not unlike a highland loch, with fine purple mountains at the head and high land along the shores.

On a spit of sand which divides a small lake from the bay, the Goletta, or fortified port is situated. There we landed and went to see the ruins of Carthage, about two miles distant. On a hill surrounded by a wall is enclosed the tomb of Saint Louis, erected by order of Louis Philippe in 1840. There are also several remnants of ancient sculpture built into panelled recesses under cover. Near the foot of this hill towards the sea are the remains of the cisterns that contained water for the ancient city; they are of great extent, but are now filled up with rubbish and covered over by the original groined vaults that were built of small stones or pebbles, in mortar or concrete, now harder than the stones; the arches are supported by square pillars, of the same material, but with the addition of four courses of bricks 18in. square and 3in. thick, from which the arches were sprung. In the soffits of the arches are still to be seen the marks of centres on which the concrete was laid; there is no appearence of keystones, nor courses in the archwork; all was made of the same excellent concrete, of which the present hardness and tenacity are such that, where some of the pillars have been undermined and thrown down, the vaults above remain suspended over large spaces by attachment to the adjoining arches only. Another vault constructed in a similar way close to the seashore, called Queen Dido's bath, is shown, but we had not time to visit it.

No destruction can be more complete than that which has overtaken Carthage. Few traces of this once mighty city now remain; the very configuration of the land has been in a great measure changed by the river which flows close by. Great tumuli of rubbish, a few broken shafts and capitols, a fragment of coarse mosaic, occurring at long intervals, and the ruined arches of an aqueduct spanning the plain, comprise all the evidences we saw of the "Queen of the South." An air of complete desolation reigns, and if it were not for the beauty of the purple hills which gird it round, the blue sparkling sea and the transparent air, which combined would give a charm to any spot however waste, there would be little beyond the teeming thoughts which the place suggests to give interest to the site of "Magna Carthago."

It was indeed difficult to realise what such a place had been when some 700,000 inhabitants filled its streets and 300 cities owed it allegiance. An older city than Rome, her armies had rudely thundered at the very gates of the mistress of the World, and now hardly one stone stands upon another to mark the site of her palaces.

We next visited Tunis which is as dirty and ricketty an old city as exists on the face of the earth. Its streets are thronged with turbaned men of many races, and of every imaginable hue, all of whom, however, are much more provocative of admiration when viewed from a distance than when brought into close proximity. The rude jostling in the narrow lanes, which here represent streets, were anything but pleasant, from the fact that these gaudy individuals had a most unpleasant flavour of garlic and assafœtida, which rendered their presence between you and the wind anything but agreeable.

We visited the tobacco and fez manufactories, which are the sights of the place. In the former, sundry rows of men sat grinding tobacco in mortars in a very peculiar manner.

The workers were negroes of many shades of blackness; with trifling exceptions, their garments were only imaginary: their heads close shaved except a solitary lock dependent from the crown. They sat along the edge of a platform on their heels, their great feet spread out below them and with a leer which lit up their black faces and showed their white teeth and red gums as they ground savagely in their mortars. The Tunissian soldiers are vexatious ruffians. We saw a regiment of their guards at drill. The sun was intensely hot, and as they were all clothed from head to heel in bright scarlet, and whirled and rolled about in the sand, they looked like salamanders out for a day's amusement. An English officer told us he had seen a sentry at the chief gate of the city divide his attention between a vegetable stall, of which he was the sole proprietor, and his military duties. He sold his leeks craftily till some military officer came in sight, when he abandoned his mercantile pursuits, shouldered his musket, and presented arms; after which he replaced the rusty weapon in its corner by the wall, and returned to his customer to dilate upon the excellence of his turnips and leeks.

We saw several of the "Marabouts," or holy men of Tunis, who from being supposed to be under the special protection of Heaven are held in great reverence. They are all either mad, or pretend to be so. They are allowed to help themselves to what food they wish at any shop, and the proprietor takes such attention as a compliment. Several of these gentry were very fierce-looking, having long matted hair, and beards begrimed with filth. Their clothes hung in tatters from their gaunt limbs, and the scallop-shell of the pilgrim was attached to their shoulders. We were careful to imitate the natives, who obsequiously made way for these impostors as they strode about gesticulating wildly apparently at nothing.

Tunis and Tripoli formed part of the Carthaginian state and were both destroyed by the Romans 148 years B.C. Tunis was besieged by Louis IX. of France in 1270; but it remained under African kings till taken by Barbarossa, under Soliman the Magnificent. Barbarossa was expelled by Charles V.; but the country was recovered by the Turks, under Selim II. It was again taken, with great slaughter, by the Emperor Charles V., in 1535, when 10,000 Christian slaves were set at liberty. The Bey of Tunis was first appointed in 1570. But the city was reduced by Admiral Blake, on the Bey refusing to deliver up the British captives, in 1656.

Their general method of building appears to have continued the same from the earliest ages down to the present time, without the least alteration or improvement. Large doors, spacious chambers, marble pavements, cloistered courts, with fountains sometimes playing in the midst, are certainly well adapted to the circumstances of the climate. The mortar or cement they generally use, particularly where any extraordinary strength or compactness is required, appears to be of the very same composition with what may be found in the most ancient remains. The cisterns that were built by Sultan Ben Eglib in several parts of the kingdom of Tunis are of equal solidity with the celebrated ones at Carthage, and continue to this day, unless where they have been designedly broken down, as firm and compact as if they were but just finished. The mortar is made in this manner : they take one part of sand, two parts of wood ashes, and three of lime, which, after it has been well sifted and mixed together, is then beaten for three days and nights incessantly with wooden mallets, sprinkling the mortar alternately and at proper times with a little oil and water till it become of a proper consistence. This mortar is chiefly used in making arches, cisterns, and terraces for the house tops; it quickly assumes the hardness of stone, and is impervious to water. This composition is also used for covering the flat roofs of the houses in Malta.

Having arrived at Malta we hired a house, and passed through the winter in the pleasant society of former friends until the 9th of February, 1861, when at about one o'clock a.m. an earthquake took place which shook the island and caused much consternation in the city of Valetta. The vibrations were sufficiently strong to set the house-bells ringing. As nearly as I could reckon the shocks were about three in two seconds, with a noise like that produced by a waggon passing over an archway. In a few minutes nearly the whole population ran out in the streets, fled to the churches and began to ring the bells; they hurried there from all quarters, and those who could afford it made costly offerings at the shrines of the saints.

Though the earthquake had been violent, but little perceptible damage was done to the buildings. We saw at the house of a Maltese gentlemen a collection of antique curiosities found on the island at various periods; and in the public library are some curious manuscripts, such as original letters of Henry VII. of England to L'Isle Adam, and the original grant of the island by Charles V. to the Knights Templars.

Though the winter temperature at Malta is rarely

below 60° Fahrenheit, as it is perched on a rock exposed to every wind that blows, it is not a desirable place for invalids with bronchial complaints, and to keep one's rooms well heated is a matter of first necessity; but Liverpool coals can be procured at a reasonable price.

The rock which forms the substratum of the island is an excellent building material, which enables the inhabitants to erect buildings at little cost; when taken from the quarry, which is frequently the spot on which the building is erected, it can be readily cut by such saws, axes, and chisels as are used by carpenters; but when for some time exposed to the air it acquires such hardness that many large houses in Valetta, known to be nearly three hundred years old, exhibit no appearances of decay, except at the surface of the ground where the walls are alternately wet and dry.

In building, the masons cut the stone into blocks of various lengths, but of one thickness equal to that of the intended wall; all the ornamental or moulded work of the fronts is cut upon the walls after the building is roofed. The floors are supported by wooden joists placed about two feet apart, and on these joists coarse flagstones are laid, and covered with sand, upon which thin slabs of stone, square and smooth, are laid in cement, this forms the floor, which has always a very clean and cool appearance. The roof is flat and made in the same manner, except that the upper surface has a slight inclination to cast off the rain, and is covered with a cement like that already described for the cisterns and terraces at Carthage and Tunis. The water is conveyed by pipes from the roof to a cistern under the house, which gives generally a sufficient supply for all domestic purposes, except in dry seasons, when an additional supply is brought from a distance by a small aqueduct.

As there is no woodwork used in building, except the beams, doors and windows, such a thing as a house being burnt down is never heard of. In a history of Malta, it is stated that the first settlers on the island were Phœnicians. The Greeks took possession of it at an early period. The Carthaginians, under Hannibal, had it in A.M. 3620. The inhabitants were strongly attached to the Carthaginians by a common origin and language. After the first Punic war it was taken by the Romans, and, in A.D. 506, it was taken by the Goths, who held it for only 37 years, when it was taken by Belisarius, and remained under the Emperors of Constantinople till the latter part of the 9th century, It fell into the hands of the Arabs in A.D. 879, when they killed or made slaves of all the Greeks they found on the island. The inhabitants in the course of two centuries had adopted the Arab language, a dialect of which is still the spoken language of the people. In 1090, Count Roger and his brother William, took it, and expelled the Arabs; and in 1530 it passed into the hands of Charles V., who ceded it to the Knights of St. John of Jerusalem. The Turks made several attempts to get a footing on the island, but were always repulsed by the knights with severe loss

In 1565 the city was besieged by an immense Turkish force, who were after two months of desperate fighting at last beaten off, leaving behind them in killed 25,000 Turkish soldiers; the loss on the side of the Christians were 800 citizens and 260 knights.

In 1798 the island was taken by General Bonaparte on his expedition to Egypt. He found in it 1,200 cannons,

200,000 lbs. of powder, two ships of the line, a frigate, four galleys, and 40,000 muskets, besides an immense treasure and 4,500 Turkish prisoners, whom he set at liberty. Malta was blockaded by the British in 1798, and was taken by Major-general Pigot in 1800. At the peace of Amiens it was stipulated that the island should be restored to the Knights, but the British retained possession of it till 1814, when by the treaty of Paris the island was guaranteed to Great Britian. The town of Valetta being on a hill, with the principal street running north and south along the top, the cross streets which descend to the bay on either side are so steep that the sidewalks are formed into flights of steps, which are very fatiguing.

Having made preparations for a visit to Egypt, I engaged a passage by steamer from Malta to Alexandria, and reached that city among a crowd of passengers on their way to India and Australia. We landed, and, having passed through the narrow and irregular streets of the Turkish quarter, were astonished at the contrast presented by the larger and cleaner dwellings of the Europeans.

The most striking monuments of ancient Alexandria are the well-known obelisks and Pompey's Pillar. The obelisks stood originally at Heliopolis, and were brought to Alexandria by one of the Cæsars; though fame has attached to them the title of Cleopatra's Needles. They are of red granite of Syene, like most of the obelisks of Egypt. The standing obelisk is about 70 feet high, with a diameter at its base of 7 feet 7in. One is still standing, the other has been thrown down and lies close to its pedestal, which stood on two steps of white limestone. It was given by Mohammed Ali to the English, but they did not think it worth the cost and trouble of transportation. Pompey's Pillar, which stands on an eminence consists of a capital, shaft, base, and pedestal, which last reposes on substructions of smaller blocks, once belonging to older monuments; its total height is 98 feet 9 inches. A few years ago curiosity had tempted the Arabs and some Europeans to dig into and pick out the cement that united these stones, which might have endangered the safety of the column had not the Pasha ordered the holes to be filled up with mortar, to check the curious. There is a rare old book which happily throws light on what this pillar was. In the twelfth century, while the Crusaders were ravaging Syria, a learned physician of Bagdad, named Abdallatif, visited Egypt and dwelt a considerable time there. He afterwards wrote an admirable account of whatever he himself saw in the country; and his work has been translated by some Arabic scholars. The best translation is by De Sacy (Paris, 1810). — Abdallatif tells us that the column (now called Pompey's Pillar) was called by the Arabs " the pillar of the colonnades ; " that he had himself seen the remains of above four hundred columns of the same material, lying on the margin of the sea ; and he tells us how they came there. He declares that the governor of Alexandria, the officer put in charge of the city by Saladin had overthrown and broken these columns to make a breakwater ! "This," observes Abdallatif, "was the act of a child, or of a man who does not know good from evil." He continues: "I have seen, also, round the pillar of the colonnades considerable remains of these columns; some entire, others broken. It was evident from these remains that the columns had been

7

covered by a roof which they supported. Above the pillar is a cupola supported by it. I believe that this was the portico where Aristotle taught, and his disciples after him; and that this was the academy which Alexander erected when he built the city, and where the library was placed which Amrou burned by the permission of Omar."

De Sacy reminds us that the alleged destruction of this portico must have taken place, if at all, at most thirty years before the visit of Abdallatif; so that as "all the inhabitants of Alexandria, without exception," assured that traveller of the fact, it would be unreasonable to doubt it. He decides that here we have the far-famed Serapeum.

Nothing which remains of Alexandria attests its greatness more than the Catacombs upon the coast to the westward. The extent of them is remarkable; but the principal inducement to visit them is the elegance and symmetry of the architecture in one of the chambers, having a Doric entablature and mouldings, in good Greek taste, which is not to be met with in any other part of Egypt.

The circumference of ancient Alexandria is said by Pliny to have been fifteen miles, and Strabo gives it a diameter of 30 stadia. Its population amounted to more than 300,000 free inhabitants, "besides at least an equal number of slaves." Nor were the greatness and flourishing condition of Alexandria of short duration; and even as late as the year A. D. 640, when taken by the Arabs, it was remarkable for its wealth and splendour. "I have taken," says Amer in his letter to the Caliph, "the great city of the West. It is impossible for me to enumerate the variety of its riches and beauty, and I shall content myself with observing that it contains

4,000 palaces, 4,000 baths, 400 theatres or places of amusement, 12,000 shops for the sale of vegetables; and 40,000 tributary Jews.

The commanding position of Egypt in the ancient world and its comparative insignificance in modern times are two facts which equally puzzle the historian and the economist. History does not enable us to understand how a country which has thrice, at least, been the seat of a powerful empire should have again and again degenerated into a mere province. Political economy does not teach us how one of the richest valleys in the world, watered by one of the longest of rivers, open through all its length to the commerce of Europe, connected with Asia by the Isthmus of Suez and the Red sea, and inhabited by an industrious population from the earliest ages, can have been so far outstripped in wealth and civilization by nations so infinitely inferior in natural advantages. Besides, the marvel is that Egypt, so often the coveted prize of western conquerors, should never have fallen under the sway of some Christian government, instead of becoming the dependency of the only European power which is Oriental in religion and policy.

Whatever be the cause, however, the result is that, until a very recent period, the condition of Egypt had varied little from that described by Herodotus. The traveller still took the first Greek historian and the Old Testament as his manuals; he found the same agricultural system, the same degradation of the labourer, the same apathy and corruption in high places, the same incapacity for an independent destiny, which have been the stereotyped features of the Egyptian people for more than twenty centuries. Foreign merchants were to be seen at Alexandria, as Greek merchants were congregated at Naucratis; French adventurers surrounded and solicited the Pasha, as Greek adventurers used to surround and solicit Amasis and his successors; but still Egypt remained a wonder of the world, the land of physical paradoxes and colossal monuments of art, but she had lost every vestige of her former intellectual supremacy, and was incomparably feebler in military force than under the dynasties recorded in the hieroglyphics. Generations are needed to undo evils which have been maturing for generations, and though metaphors borrowed from human life have no proper application to nations, yet something analagous to the decay of rallying power seems to be experienced by races which have long ceased to have any faith in themselves.

Having seen the principal objects of interest in Alexandria, I began to make preparations for a trip up the Nile, and for that purpose hired a boat to take us to the second cataract, and back again to Cairo. The boat, though not very large, was a handsome one, and belonged to the ladies of the Pasha's harem; they did not require its use in the winter, so they let it out for that season. There was a regular crew of fourteen men, a reis, or captain, and a pilot, all dressed in a sort of uniform, who were attached to and were let along with the boat. The men in leisure hours formed themselves into a sort of musical band, with rude instruments composed chiefly of small drums and triangles, to which they chanted songs that were not disagreeable when one became used to them. Under the advice of an experienced friend, I engaged as dragoman Hassan Ismael, who had for several years acted in that capacity with various other travellers. I entered into a written contract with him, by which he engaged to furnish all necessary provisions of every kind, to defray all costs and charges of the boat and the crew, from Cairo to the second cataract and back again ; to visit all such towns and antiquities along both sides of the Nile as I might desire to see, to stop or go forward whenever I desired it, that the trip should occupy three months, and that Hassan himself, as well as every person belonging to the boat, were at all times to be under my control for the three months.

We left Alexandria by railway for Cairo, and reached that place in six hours. It is at Cairo we begin to feel that we are in the wonderful East,—the scene of the most marvellous incidents in the history of the world. At Alexandria and on the railway route we see that we are upon Oriental ground—the palm trees, the customs and appearance of the people, the peculiar language, are all very suggestive; but it is at Cairo that we are introduced to a description of life of which we have only been able to form a vague idea from books. There is so little difference in the character of the cities of the East, ruled over and inhabited by Mahometans, that at Cairo we may suppose ourselves at Bagdad, Bassorah, or Damascus.

All the characters of the "Arabian Nights" and other Eastern romances flit by us in turn. The custom of baksheesh— begged for by so many of the people gives much annoyance to travellers ; the study of the numerous types of the mixed population is not without interest. The public promenades at the citadel give ample opportunities for that purpose. From the top of its terraces can be seen the thousand narrow streets of a city containing more than 200,000 inhabitants, with the pyramids of Gizeh in the distance towards the west.

In the centre is a green spot, the Esbikir, a walk formed by Mehemet Ali. On all sides are seen mosques of Moorish architecture with lofty minarets. At your feet are the tombs of the Caliphs and Mamelukes — square monuments surmounted by semi-spherical domes. A principal object of attraction is the Egyptian Museum; in the entrance court of which are some fine sarcophagi of pink granite, in which were laid the boxes, made of sycamore and covered with hieroglyphic inscriptions, that contained the mummies wrapped up in their manifold bandages; some of these cases are of great richness, and a glass case near them contains the different jewellery, such as necklaces, earrings, chains, and bracelets in massive gold, that were placed on the body of each queen of the dynasties of the Pharaohs. The collections of scarabéei are unique in the world. The objects in bronze, representing Egyptian divinities, are in excellent preservation; the terra cottas of a blueish and greenish tint have the most fantastic forms; and the charming scentbottles in jasper and cornelian excite the envy of many fair visitors.

Within the enclosure to the citadel, is placed Joseph's Well; it is a sunk shaft, cut down in the solid sandstone to a depth of 280 feet. Around this shaft is a spiral stairway descending to about 150 feet, between which and the shaft is a partition of eight inches thick of the solid rock, in which at certain distances openings were cut to give light and air from the shaft to the stairway. At this depth of 150 feet, there is a circular space excavated for a horizontal wheel worked by mules; this wheel drives another, on the periphery of which a series of earthen pots attached to an endless rope go down to the bottom empty on one side, dip into the water below and come up full on the opposite side. From this platform the water is raised by a similar wheel worked by oxen, and discharged into a tank on the surface of the ground. I tasted of the water, and found it to be of good quality.

The Mamelukes, a dynasty that reigned for a considerable time in Egypt, were originally Turkish and Circassian slaves, and were established in Egypt by the Sultan Saladin as a kind of body guard in A.D. 1246. They after some time conspired, and advanced one of their own corps to the throne of Egypt, and this they continued to do until the country became a Turkish province in 1517, when the beys took them into pay, and filled up their ranks as they became vacant with renegades from various countries. On the conquest of Egypt by Bonaparte in 1798, they retreated into Nubia, where they remained, until, assisted by the Arnauts who were introduced into the country by the war, the Mamelukes once more wrested Egypt from the Turkish government. In 1811, they were decoyed by the Turkish pasha to a feast in the citadel at Cairo, and were there all cruelly murdered, except one man, who alone escaped from the building, flew to his horse, dashed full speed to a gap in the outer wall, sprung over it and descended into the road below, a depth of 120 feet, landing upon a pile of soft rubbish; the horse was killed, but the man escaped with life, and by the assistance of friends got clear off into the country. This was the only one of all his companions who escaped that terrible slaughter.

On our way back to the hotel we saw a blind Arab, one of those famed story-tellers of the East standing in an open space, surrounded by a crowd of listeners seated upon their heels in a circle, all deeply interested in his story, which we were told was something in the style of the Arabian Nights' Entertainments.

We visited the grand mosque of Mehemet Ali, built entirely of Oriental alabaster, after the model of Saint Sophia at Constantinople, and therein saw his tomb, in form like a sarcophagus two stories in height, covered with silk, and Arabic inscriptions in letters and ornaments of gold.

We made an excursion to Heliopolis, that famous city where Plato was said to have studied for thirteen years under the priests of the temple of the sun. There is nothing now remaining of that once magnificent temple but one of the two obelisks that stood at its entrance, the other was many years ago removed to Alexandria, where it now lies prostrate, half buried in the sand, and is every day becoming less by the chipping process of enthusiastic tourists. There are three stones that have been raised out of the sand at the temple, on one of which there are hieroglyphic writings; these are all that can be seen at present belonging to the temple.

There is an old sycamore tree in the neighbourhood, of which the Arabs have a legend, that the holy family on the " flight into Egypt" once reposed under its branches. It is evidently a very old tree, though still covered with foliage.

The well that belonged to the temple, still supplies excellent water to the few inhabitants of the place. The road from Cairo to Heliopolis passes through a sandy desert for a great portion of the way; it also passes by the palace of Aboozabel Pasha, where there is a tall tower of five storeys which was formerly used as a telegraph station.

We went to visit the mosque of the dancing dervishes,

which is a large square apartment, covered by a semi-spherical dome; and saw their peculiar mode of worship, which is an extraordinary thing to witness. They placed themselves round in a circle upon the floor, and commenced the performance by groaning, and calling on Allah, which they repeated slowly but with much emphasis, bending forward the body at each repetition, and increasing the rapidity of the motion as they went on, until after some time a handsome young priest, dressed in a flowing robe of violet silk and a tall cap of the same material on his head, entered the circle and with arms extended began to turn round slowly at first, with a monotonous chant, but gradually increasing the movement until he at last spun round with astonishing velocity and sank down finally in total exhaustion. The other worshippers again commenced as at first, calling slowly on Allah, and at each call bending the body forward so as to touch the floor with their fingers: this motion continued to increase in rapidity until perspiration fell from their faces like rain, and some at length sank to the floor in a state of total exhaustion and partial delirium. This, together with portions of the Koran read or chanted by a priest, constituted the whole of the worship on that occasion.

We next visited the Shoubra gardens, which are handsomely laid out and planted. The palace of the Pasha is not very magnificent, but the inside is fitted up and ornamented in gorgeous taste; the floors of the principal rooms are made of a dark wood, beautifully inlaid with ornaments cut out of white wood and polished until they shine like a mirror. Around the walls were placed beautiful divans stuffed with wool and covered with silk brocade. The chairs were neatly formed, white in colour, varnished, ornamented with gilding and covered with yellow satin. The windows had transparent blinds and silk curtains. The ceilings were panelled and ornamented with gilt fillagree work. There were two large mirrors in each room. In one room was a full-length portrait of Mehemet Ali, and a smaller one of his son on horseback.

On riding out to Old Cairo, which is a very rough and dilapidated place, we saw in the distance the Nilometer, which is simply a brick tower inside of which is placed a pillar with graduated marks to indicate from day to day the height of the water when the river is rising. We went into an old Coptic church, which is a rude structure, having hung round the inside coloured prints of the Virgin and Child, the Flight into Egypt, etc. There was a crypt, like a rough cellar, which contained a rude baptismal font; and a recess in the wall, which they called the Tomb of the Virgin. We were surrounded by groups of women and children, who as usual vociferated baksheesh, and followed us for a considerable distance.

Having completed our preparations at Cairo, we embarked in the boat I had procured for our voyage up the Nile; but finding a south wind blowing against us, we soon cast anchor for the night. The next morning, the wind being still ahead, the men towed the boat along the bank, which was severe and tedious work, while we landed, and walking along the margin, observed how water is raised from the river for irrigation. This occupation, together with tending a few sheep and goats, appears to be at this season the chief employment of the people. It is usual with excursionists on the Nile, to take advantage of the north wind which prevails at this season, to pass upward as quickly as they can, leaving all sightseeing until their return down with the stream.

Hassan, our dragoman, says that the inhabitants along this part of the river living in villages have to pay the government a certain tax; while, distributing among themselves whatever remains in hand, they divide this in proportion to the number of each family, and thus they contrive to subsist till the next season. When their crops are planted, having then nothing to do but water them, the men meet together in social circles tell stories, sing songs, pray, dance and make merry. The women spin the flax and wool on the old hand-spindle; the men weave it into cloth on the most primitive of looms, like those used by the ancient Egyptians. They know nothing about the days of the week, have neither mosque nor priest, and yet pray regularly five times a day. Each family has but one room in its mud hut, no furniture but a jar for water, an earthen pot for cooking, and an oven for baking. Their bed, of which there is but one for the whole family, consists of a piece of coarse rug spread upon the mud floor.

November 21st.— A strong north wind drove us merrily forward during the night; passing Beni Souef, we reached Shekh-em-Barak at eight o'clock in the morning. This is an immense sandhill, stratified, and partially hardened into stone. The cold north wind, blowing fiercely, caused much suffering to our crew, as their clothing is but a cotton shirt, and a loose outer garment of the same texture.

November 23d. — We this morning reached Gebel-Aboufeda —a long range of rocky precipices near the river, having caves of various forms and dimensions cut into the rocks. The food of our crew is very simple, consisting of coarse wheaten bread, cut into small pieces and dried in the air till it is hard as a brick. They make a kind of soup, which is nothing but water and salt, with any kind of green-stuff they can pick up along the bank; into this, when boiling, they put as much of the-bread as makes a mess for the whole crew; when cooked, the stew is turned into a large wooden bowl, which is placed flat on the deck, and around it the crew sit on their heels, each one having a piece of bread for a spoon dips this into the bowl and raises a portion of the stew to his mouth. They quickly finish their meal, wash their hands and mouths, and then pass round from one to the other a pipe of tobacco, of which each one takes a few whiffs. They take but two meals a day, morning and evening.

For about two miles the face of the rocks at this place is excavated into caves of various shapes and sizes. Are these the caves wherein the early Christians concealed themselves from their Roman persecutors, thus giving rise to the first examples of monastic life?

November 24th. — We reached the city of Osioot, the residence of the Governor of Upper Egypt, which is said to contain 20,000 inhabitants. The town is about a mile from the river, and we rode to it upon donkeys. Having looked at what are called the streets, formed by mud huts on either side, we rode about a mile further back from the town to the mountain, the vertical face of which is from 80 to 100 feet high, and into this excavations have been made, some of which are 60 feet deep, 30 wide, and 20 high. In the largest cave the ceiling is flat, ornamented by fretwork, and a few lines of hieroglyphics; a few figures of men are carved upon the sides; but all are now much defaced and worn away. In the floor are several pits, where the mummies of dogs and wolves were deposited. A fine view of the fertile lands between this point and the river is obtained from the top of the rock. On our return through the city we visited a bazaar, which is a good deal like those we saw at Alexandria and Cairo.

November 25th. — We remained all day here to give the crew an opportunity for baking their bread at the public ovens, and for washing their clothes. While walking in the evening along the river's bank, I observed carpenters at work, caulking a boat; their tools are those which are used everywhere for such purposes. The chief difference is that the men sit down while at work, and this habit appears general with all mechanics. I saw a blacksmith's shop, where a small anvil was supported by a spike driven into the mud floor; the bellows being a sheepskin bag, which the man moved up and down by one hand, admitting the air by a hole, stopped by his finger at one end, and a pipe at the other end, through which the air was blown into the fire when the bag was pressed downward. I observed also that masons, while building a wall of sun-dried bricks, were seated on the top of the wall while at work.

November 26th. — This morning we took on board a queer old Arab, who left his own boat, being attracted to ours by the charms of the music of our crew; he seemed in ecstasy, and danced about in a most ludicrous manner. He was so droll that every word he uttered threw our men into fits of laughter; and on landing in the evening at his own village, he entreated us to take pipes and coffee, but as this would have occasioned too much delay we declined it.

November 27th. — We passed a Coptic monastery inclosed by a brick wall surrounding a square; above the wall, were several small domes which covered the buildings within. The monastery is beautifully situated.

November 28th. — We passed the town of Girgeh

at dusk ; our boat grounding on a sandbank, from which our men had great difficulty in getting her off. This is our twelfth day from Cairo, and we have made no more than 400 miles.

November 30th.—We arrived at Kenneh, where some boats were lying, one bearing the French flag; while our men went to the town to buy tobacco and other necessaries, I landed for a walk. I observed the cotton plant growing here, the bushes being seven or eight feet high. A store of coals is kept at this place for the use of the Pasha's steamers. We greatly rejoiced the crew by giving them a sheep, the cost of which was but 50 piastres, or eight shillings.

December 1st. — The changes of temperature are so sudden and so great, that I have taken a severe cold by which I am much distressed.

December 2d. — On passing a small village to day, we heard loud cries of lamentation. I landed, taking Hassan with me, and found that the tumult arose from the circumstance of a man having died; the body was just buried and his wives were performing a customary ceremony over the grave. I looked over a wall unobserved by them for some time. There were about twenty women screaming and dancing to the beating of a small drum, their hair hanging over their shoulders, their faces painted blue and red, and their bodies begrimed with dust — the most wild and revolting spectacle I ever witnessed. When they at last observed me, they were very much enraged and ordered me away, an order I was willing enough to obey.

December 3d. — We arrived at Luxor, where we found letters for us at the post-office. We remained here throughout the day, in order to finish and send off our letters to Cairo, as this will be our last opportunity for some time.

December 4th. — We reached Esna, where we found the boat Topsy at anchor, with the flag of the United States flying. Our reis and crew went to the town in grand toilet; we are to remain here for thirty hours for the baking of bread. Many of the inhabitants have squatted on the bank to indulge in the luxury of a stare at us and our boat; they all look and dress alike. We landed for the purpose of visiting a fine temple at this place. The interior of it was formerly completely filled with sand blown in from the desert, but in 1823 it was cleared out by orders from Mehemet Ali: it is now fast filling again. The length of the interior is about one hundred feet, by fifty feet wide, and twenty feet high; there are three rows of beautiful columns, six in each row, all finely formed, with highly ornamented capitals, each differing in design from the others. The ceiling is covered with hieroglyphic writings in a tolerably good state of preservation.

December 7th. — We had a good run with a fair wind all night, and have made 70 miles; the country through which we passed is poor and barren. We reached Assouan, at the First Cataract.

December 8th. — The present town of Assouan is on the bank, while the old town, which is a ruin, is on a high mound. We walked about two miles to see the ancient granite quarries, where the material used by the ancients for all their massive works was obtained. Among many short blocks 1 observed one enormous piece, which appears to have been intended for an obelisk, still lying in the quarry only partially detached from the solid mass; these blocks all show marks of the tools used in cutting the deep grooves at certain distances along the lines of separation, wherein metallic wedges were driven to split and separate the pieces from one another, similar to the methods used in other countries at the present day. The surfaces of the blocks, though exposed to the air for so many centuries look as fresh and clean as if they had only lain there a few years. This must be attributed to the total absence of rain and frost. We returned to the town by a detour, which brought us to a small oasis, with a well of good water in the centre, and a few date trees growing round it. We waited all the evening for a man who is called the captain of the cataract, as he is to sign a contract before the governor to take our boat safely up the cataract to-morrow without damage for a certain sum.

December 9th. — We set out at 8 a.m. towards the cataract, passing between large blocks of dark rock like lava, piled up on either side of our boat in the most fantastic shapes ; we passed forward before a light wind till we arrived at the lowest torrent, which was not very rapid. The men of the cataract having fastened strong ropes round the rocks at the top of the torrent, which had a fall of not more than four of five feet in a hundred yards, the men in our boat hauled her by these ropes against the torrent, and when near the first station, shifted the ropes to other rocks farther up the stream, and by gradually shifting the ropes from point to point, the boat was finally pulled to the top of the cataract. The noise made by these men, running and jumping from rock to rock in a state of complete nudity, and shouting to one another at the highest pitch of their voices in the most frantic manner, presented the wildest scene I ever witnessed. Having arrived at a spot where there was smooth water the men would work no more that day, so there we had to remain for the night.

December 10th. — At 9 a. m., having procured an additional number of men, the boat was safely hauled to the top of the cataract, and at 1 p. m. we reached the Island of Philæ, and entered into Nubia.

December 11th. — We landed and walked on the margin of the river in front of three villages, each numbering from twenty to thirty huts. The people appeared very much poorer here than below the cataract; the boys, and even some of the girls, ran quite naked; all are as black as negroes, but have not the woolly hair nor flat noses. The Nubian language, which is exclusively spoken here, is not understood by the Arabs. They possess only a narrow strip of arable land along the river; all extending back from that is nothing but sandy desert. Their land produces any kind of vegetables they may choose to plant, but their chief dependence is a grain called *Dorra*, which appears something between wheat and rye. They have date trees along the river bank, dates being the chief production they have for sale. Their principal employment appears to be raising water from the river for irrigation, which is sometimes done by wheels worked by oxen, but oftener by manual labour. For each one of these wheels, they are forced to pay the government a tax of 400 piastres, about four pounds sterling per year.

December 12th. — We have this morning passed by two temples; there are heaps of stone near one of them that appear to have lain there since the erection of the temple. In the evening our boat having anchored by the side of a flat sandbank, the crew had for an hour a game at jump frog, which they performed very gracefully.

December 13th. — We landed and walked for an

8

hour on the margin of the desert; the people are very poor, and nearly naked, the children quite so ; they called out as we passed, Hawajah, baksheesh, and to one another " look at the lady with a dress on. "

December 14th. — It appears strange that though now within the tropics, the wind is still cold and penetrating, the thermometer in our cabin with the sun shining full upon us, and the windows shut, stands at from only 50 to 60° in the morning; and at two o'clock p. m. does not exceed 70°. In the evening, the boat struck heavily on a rock ; the reis, in a rage, thrashed the men into the water, where after much labour and floundering about they succeeded in getting off without damage into deep water, and anchored to the bank for the night.

December 15th. — We first arrived at Korosko, and there heard that a Frenchman, an M. D., was confined in prison at Derr, for having by accident a few days before shot one of the natives at this place ; and that he cannot be released until an order from Cairo to that effect can be obtained, for which a special messenger was despatched on a dromedary some days ago.

December 16th. — We came up with the boat Clotilda, and made the acquaintance of its occupants ; in the evening they returned our visit.

December 17th. — We arrived at Derr, the principal city of Nubia, which consists of mud-built-houses, surrounded by a great number of date trees.

I took Hassan and went to see the hall of justice, where the governor, the chief judge, and the principal men in office were sitting in council. The hall was a mud hut about 30 feet long, and 14 feet wide. An elevated divan, built of mud, about three feet wide, and covered by a coarse rug, extended along one side and both ends of the hall; there where two doorways, but no windows. Hassan entered with me; the governor returned my salutation, and having inquired of Hassan who I was, and where I was going, he invited me to take a seat beside him on the divan, where he was seated crosslegged. The judge and the officers were seated in a similar manner at the opposite end of the room. Pipes and coffee in the usual way were brought in and offered to us; after which, I returned thanks, made a salaam and retired. The court, and the whole of its material arrangements, appeared about as respectable as a cowshed, and yet in the manner and bearing of the governor there was a greater degree of dignity and ease than one could expect to meet in such a place. We went onward again, and in the evening anchored by the side of the Clotilda.

December 18th.—We had a fair wind to-day and the two boats went on side by side very pleasantly, passing the ruined town of Ibreem, and the grand temples of Aboo Simbel with their gigantic statues, which we shall examine on our return. We arrived in the evening at Wadee Halfeh, the highest point on the Nile to which travellers' boats ascend.

December 20th.—A cold north wind is blowing keenly. I took Hassan to the house of the government agent, whom we found squatted on the ground in an open court, with two tax-collectors that were paying over to him the taxes collected by them from two villages. I saw at this place several traders' boats that come up the Nile to take in at this place the bales and packages of gum, ivory tusks, and senna, which are brought from various places in the interior of Africa on the backs of camels, and delivered to these traders, who take them to Cairo and Alexandria.

December 21st.—Mounted on donkeys, we ascended by the side of the cataract, to Abooseer — a high rock at a distance of six miles from our boat; from which an extensive view to the horizon all round is obtained ; towards the south, mountain tops are seen in the distance, cloud-like and indistinct; on all other sides there is nothing but the sandy desert, excepting the cataract, which for a distance of three or four miles is studded whith masses of dark rocks, that look like gigantic lumps of coal, strewn about in the greatest confusion, between which the waters of the Nile tumble down in admired disorder. This point is the ultimate distance to which excursionists usually ascend on the Nile. The rock is of gray sandstone, and every smooth foot of its surface is covered with the names of visitors ; but I saw none bearing an earlier date than 1824. To comply with the common practice I recorded our names among the others. On our return we came upon several encampments of those Nubian traders who formerly, among other articles of traffic, brought numbers of young slaves, kidnapped in the interior, and sent them down to Cairo. I was told that there are still a few slaves smuggled down the river, though it is at present contrary to law.

December 24th.—At 4 a.m. the head of our boat was turned northward amidst as much noise, singing, and music, as the crew could in any possible way get up ; they rowed down stream against the wind to Aboo-Simbel, where we anchored close to the Clotilda.

The two temples of Aboo-Simbel are both of the time of Ramases II.; nothing more interesting than these temples is to be found beyond the limits of Thebes. Of the six statues of the facade, the two in the centre represent Athor, whose calm and gentle face is surmounted by a crown with the moon contained within the cow's horns. The excavation of this temple was performed nearly 1400 B. C. The temple extends from the portal, about ninety feet into the rock. On the walls are figured men of the old military caste, in their defensive armour — a sort of cuirass of chain work — red links on a yellow ground; the civilians in red frocks and the women in tight yellow garments, with red sashes tied in front. The entrance hall is supported by six square pilasters, all of which bear the head of Athor. The plain surfaces are everywhere covered with engraved figures or hieroglyphic writings.

Of the colossi in front of the large temple, the southernmost is the only complete one. The next to it is much shattered; the other two have each lost the top of the helmet. They are much sanded up : the sand slopes up from the half cleared entrance to the chin of the most northern figure; part of the lower jaw, reaching half-way up to the lower lip, was composed of the mud and straw of which crude bricks are made. There had been evidently a fault in the stone, which was supplied by this material. It was most beautifully moulded. The beauty of the curves of these great faces is surprising in the fidelity of the rounding of the muscles and the grace of the flowing lines of the cheek and jaw; a difficult task in the case of a statue seventy feet high standing up against the face of a rock. On the legs of the shattered colossus are Greek letters, composing an inscription by the soldiers sent by Psammitichus in pursuit of the soldiers who deserted from his service. It is a mistake to suppose that the expression of a face must be injured by its features being colossal. In Egypt it may be seen that a mouth three feet wide may be as delicate, and a nostril which spans a foot as sensitive in expression as in any marble bust of our day.

Abdallatif, seven hundred years ago, left us his testimony as follows, in speaking of the Sphinx :—" A little more than a bow-shot from the pyramids we see a colossal head and neck appearing above ground. Its countenance is very charming, and its mouth gives an impression of sweetness and beauty. An able man having asked me what I admired most of all I had seen in Egypt, I told him that it was the truth of the head of the Sphinx. "

December 26th. — When we had prepared to leave Aboo Simbel, it was found that one of the crew was missing; the reis sent men to look for him in all directions,—he was nowhere to be found; but we dropped down the river a short distance, and anchored for the night. There was a village a few miles above Aboo-Simbel, and the reis sent a party, headed by his brother, to this village, to which it appeared the poor man had wandered, and falling in with a gang of thieves they had stripped him of his clothes and confined him in one of their hovels.

The leader of our party, being able to speak the Nubian language, inquired for the sheik of the village, told him our boat belonged to the Pasha, and that if the missing man were not safely given up, the sheik and all the inhabitants of the village should be fined and subjected to dreadful punishment. This threat had the desired effect, the man's clothing was restored, and he returned to the boat.

December 27th. — We passed down to Derr; the

Frenchman was still kept a close prisoner in his boat, but had his firearms restored by the governor, as a protection from attack by the relations of the dead man. The poor prisoner was in danger of being starved, as the natives would sell him no provisions of any kind; we presented him with a small stock of things from our store, for which he was very thankful. The temple at Derr is an excavation in the rock, containing a few figures and hieroglyphics, not worthy of much admiration. We then passed down to the temple of Amada, which is of the time of Ramases II., and is built of blocks of sandstone; the figures and writings on the interior are of the best style of art we have yet seen. We then dropped farther down, and anchored close by a boat belonging to an English family on their way upward.

December 28th.—A fine calm morning, the rowers were early at work. We reached Sabooa and visited its temple, which was once a magnificent structure, but is now much dilapidated, and nearly filled with sand : it had two rows of sphinxes, each numbering eight figures, in front of the building; and four statues, two on the front, and one at each side; but all are now in a state of ruin.

December 29th.—We visited at Kortee a ruin of the time of the Romans, built of blocks of stone taken from older buildings; the foundation of the front, and of one side, have given way, and the superincumbent walls have fallen outward; there are still standing two walls and several columns, with their capitals, each differing in design from the others; portions of the architraves and cornice are left on the top.

We next visited the temple of Dakkeh, which had

once been a beautiful specimen of architecture and carving. I observed here, that in constructing the walls, the joints of the stones were fitted to one another with great accuracy, and that in the horizontal joints, a square groove was cut half in each block, which when filled with cement made a tongue or key which prevented the blocks from sliding upon one another; their ends were secured by dovetailed clamps of metal; but these clamps have all been taken out, and it would seem that to get them away, the stones have been broken and the walls destroyed.

December 30th.—One of our crew is a negro; the poor fellow had a convulsive fit last night, brought on by exposure to the cold wind without sufficient clothing. We have this day visited the temple of Gerf Hossayn, and also that of Dendoor, but neither of them excite much interest.

December 31st.—We reached the temple of Kalabshee, which presents the largest ruin of any in Nubia, and was built in the times of the Cæsars; the stones of which it was formed belonged to an older edifice. The sculptures were not in the best style; there was much colouring used upon the figures and in the writings.

At Wadee Tafa and at Gertasse there are remains of small temples, not of sufficient importance to merit description. I bought at this place a lump of what the people called petrified sponge, found among the ruins at Kalabshee. In the evening, we visited the temple of Isis at Dabod.

January 1st, 1858.— We reached the island of Philæ this morning. It is no less interesting from the subjects contained in its sacred buildings than from the scenery of the adjoining island, and the wild rocks on the opposite shore, which have obtained the epithet " beautiful." The principal building on the island is the temple of Isis. The eastern tower of the inner propylon stands on a granite rock; many parts of the building, particularly the portico, are remarkable for lightness and elegance; and from the state of their preservation they convey a good idea of the effect of colour combined with the details of architecture. Nor are the sculptures void of interest, especially those of the chamber over the western adytum containing the death and resurrection of Osiris, as well as the birth of Horus, which throw much light on the study of Egyptian mythology. This youthful deity, with his parents, Isis and Osiris, constituted the triad worshipped at Philæ. We visited the ruins by moonlight, when they presented a ghostlike and most interesting appearance.

January 2d.—We made an attempt at 8 this morning to descend the cataract, but the north wind blew so fiercely we were obliged to postpone our descent and wait for a calmer hour. We took the small boat and returned to Philæ to visit the remains of an ancient temple on the small island of Biggeh, which is said to be of the time of Ramases II., but there is not much more than two columns remaining. There is part of a granite statue seated in a chair, but it has lost the head. The few remaining sculptures and writings are in a style superior to even those of Philæ.

Hassan has been occupied all the evening in making arrangements with the captain of the cataract to take us down to-morrow.

January 3d. — Our boat was crowded at daybreak by the captain and men of the cataract, preparing for our descent ; the noise was again as terrific as it was on our ascent. We started at 7 a.m. by a shorter but more rapid course; the rush down was alarming from its rapidity, and until we reached the bottom of the torrent and turned sharply round into smooth water the excitement was intense. Hassan was obliged to give away his turban, shawls, and several smaller things to the men of the cataract; without which, they would on Hassan's next visit probably destroy his boat, for they are a horrid set of ruffians.

January 4th. — We started this morning at 8 a.m., but, after rowing against the wind for a couple of hours, we were obliged to anchor and wait for calmer weather.

January 6th. — We passed Silsileh, and rowed on against a fierce gale of north wind, until we reached Edfoo, where we visited the temples, which are very grand, and if cleared of the sand and rubbish would present magnificent examples of architecture and sculpture. On our return to the boat, we saw a pair of muzzled oxen treading out corn, as was the practice thousands of years ago; the oxen were tied to a stake driven into the threshing floor, from which a rope kept them in the circle around which they walked; the heads of corn were placed in the circuit, to a depth of about four inches, and it required about two hours to trample out the grain of one floor.

We then descended the river to the grottoes of Eilethyas, which are situated about half a mile from the river. There is only one of them in a tolerable state of preservation; it is cut out of the rock about 25 feet deep, 10 feet high, and 10 feet wide. The ceiling is semi-circular, the surface appears to have been coated with plaster on which figures were engraved and coloured, to represent the various employments of an agricultural population.

January 8th. — We arrived at Esné, where our men prepared a sufficient quantity of bread to last them till they reach Cairo. A number of dancing girls and a musician came alongside of our boat, but as they found no encouragement to remain they soon took their departure. We visited the palace and gardens of the Pasha at this place, which are but mean and inconvenient. The Pasha is expected here to-morrow, so that his baths are heated and ready for him at any moment.

January 10th. — The bread having been brought on board, we started at 11 a.m., and at 8 p.m. anchored for the night; a boat brought us some fish as large as salmon, which for four fish cost 30 piastres, equal to five shillings ; but we found them coarse and without flavour.

January 12th. — We reached Luxor, and received our letters.

Those that have not seen El-Karnac know nearly as much as can be told by those who have — that here are the largest buildings and the most extensive ruins in the known world; that the great hall is 329 feet long, 170 wide, and 85 high, containing 134 columns, and 12 central ones which are 12 feet in diameter, and the others not much smaller; the whole of this forest of columns are gay with colours, and studded with sculptures. — Of this hall the central roof is gone, and part of the lateral covering. The columns are falling ; there is nitre in the stone, and the occasional damps from the ground cause the corrosion of these mighty masses near the bases. They fall one by one ; and these leaning wrecks, propped up by some accident which must give way, have a very mournful aspect. A stone has fallen out in more than one place from the wall of the old propyla ; and looking in at the holes, sculptured and painted blocks can be seen built into the interior, remnants of an older structure, These propyla were built before Moses was born. The great hall was built by Osirei; but the original buildings of El-Karnac are of a date far beyond our knowledge. The earliest portions now remaining are a hundred years older than any other edifices in Thebes. The only known allusion to the Jews in the monuments of Egypt is on the walls of El-Karnac. The conqueror Sheshonk (Shishak) holds by the hair a group of captives, whose race is determined, not only by the face, but by the cities of Judah being named in writing among the array of tributaries.

We crossed to the Lybian side of the river, and pass-ed onward to the pair of colossi sitting alone on the plain. The impressions of sublime tranquillity they convey when seen from distant points is confirmed by a near approach. There they sit on their thrones, hands on knees, gazing straight forward, seeming, though so much of the faces is gone, to be looking over to the monumental piles on the other side of the river, which became gorgeous temples after these throne seats were placed here — the most immoveable thrones that have ever been established on earth. The figure which is popularly called Memnon, " that at sunrise played, " is sadly shattered. This is the work that Cambyses tried to overthrow, but which by all his efforts he only succeeded in shattering down to the waist. It is patched up again, a blank rough space only remain-ing where the face should be. If the faces were of the tranquil character that marks those at Aboo-Simbel, the impression must have been majestic indeed : inviolable to any one but Cambyses.

These statues sit now, at the season when travellers visit them, in the midst of an expanse of verdure. At high Nile they are islands in the midst of a waste of waters.

But of old their pedestals rose from the pavement of
the dromos, or course, which formed the avenue to the
palace-temple of Amunoph, eleven hundred feet behind
the colossi.   This palace-temple, once superb with its
statues, columns and sphinxes, is now a mere heap of
ruins.   The sphinxes are at Saint Petersburgh ; the statues peep out in fragments from under the soil.   In the
days of the glory of Thebes, the Nile did not come up
here ; but the whole avenue, with all its erections, stood
on raised ground.   The Nile itself has risen since those
days ; and in proportion to the raising of its bed has
been the spread over the plain ; so that the pavement of
the dromos, and the pedestals of the colossi, have been
buried deeper and deeper in mud; and must continue
to be so.   These statues now stand fifty-three feet above
the soil, and seven feet below it (1) ; but the mention of
their total height gives less idea of their magnitude than
the measurement of the limbs.   From the elbow to the
fingers' ends, they measure seventeen feet nine inches;
and from the knee to the plant of the foot nineteen
feet eight inches.

To-day we saw, for the first time, an old Egyptian
palace; that of Ramases the Great, so many of whose
monuments we had visited higher up the river.   This
palace of the Ramaseum (commonly called the Mem-
nonium) is also a temple.   The old Pharaohs brought
their gods into their palaces, so that the great buildings
were appropriated to gods and kings jointly.   Here in
the propylon lies the statue of the king, the largest statue that even Egypt ever produced.   It is only from a
distance that this mass of granite would be perceived to
be a statue, so enormous is its bulk.   It lies overthrown

_____

(1) The pedestals are 34 1/2 feet long, 17 3/4 wide, and 14 feet high,
making about 8,573 cubic feet.

among the fragments of its limbs; the foot looks like a block preparing for a colossal statue. I had the curiosity to measure the second toe, and found its length to be two feet seven inches. Some travellers have mounted up to the head by setting their feet in the hieroglyphic letters on its back. The features are gone, the greater part of the face being split away for millstones by the Arabs! How such a mass of syenite granite could have been transported here is wonderful, the means employed for its ruin are scarcely less wonderful; the throne and legs are completely destroyed, and reduced to comparatively small fragments, while the upper part, broken to the waist, is merely thrown back upon the ground, and lies in that position which was the consequence of its fall; nor are there any marks of the wedge or other instrument, which should have been employed for reducing those fragments to the state in which they now appear. Its overthrow is probably coeval with the Persian invasion. To say that this is the largest statue in Egypt will convey no idea of the gigantic size or enormous weight of a mass, which from an approximate calculation, exceeded, when entire, eight hundred and eighty seven tons. How should we now set about quarrying and transporting such a mass from a distance of some hundreds of miles?

The lighting of the hall of the palace was beautiful. The roof in the centre was elevated some feet above the lateral roofing: so that large oblong spaces were left for a sight of the blue sky; and when they admitted the slanting rays of the rising and setting sun upon this grove of pillars, and through them lighted up the pictured walls, the glory must have been great. Forty-eight pillars supported these roofs — roofs which were painted starry and blue like the sky. The hall was one hundred feet long. Beyond it extended pillared chambers in succession and in groups till we come upon mere traces of their walls and bases of their columns, and at last out upon the bare rock.

We visited to-day a very beautiful temple at El-Kurneh. It is old, being begun by the father of the great Ramases, in honour of *his* father; and completed by his son in honour of himself.

When the Pharaohs built their palaces and temples, they had more aims than one to fulfil. They blazoned their own deeds upon them; but they glorified the deeds of their fathers, even more carefully than their own; and they must have had in view the sympathy and edification of other men, living and to live. But their careful choice and elaborate preparation of their tombs, with every possible resort in the employment of them, show us that the unseen state was the most interesting subject, and the firmest faith in them. The Pharaohs were wont to devote the early years of their reigns to royal deeds of rule and conquest, and they did not begin to build their palaces and temples till they had achieved deeds with which to glorify them, and brought home captives to do the work of building them. But it was quite otherwise with their tombs. Every man who could afford himself a tomb began its preparation early in life. A palace or a temple could be carried on to completion by a successor; but a tomb was sealed up when the owner was laid in it. Few or none appear to be finished in every part; and some were in progress through a long course of years. The way to the long home of the Theban kings is very appropriate: a succession of winding defiles between desolate rocks, in the still congregation of this deep valley. To the old Egyptians as to others, every man must have felt himself one of a very small company in comparison with that which he was to join, in the realms of the dead. But the case of the kings was strong indeed. Each one of them lived solitary when alive; it was only when he died that he could enter among his peers. To him this was the great event to which he was looking forward during the best years of his life; and he devoted his wealth, his thoughts, and the most sacred desires of his heart to the preparation for his promotion to the society of kings and the presence of the gods. There an abode would be prepared for him. On the walls of his tomb he attempted to paint the succession of mansions in the great heavenly house which he was to inhabit at last; but meanwhile he was to dwell for a vast length of time, in the long home in the valley where his peers were lying still all round about him. Every Egyptian king was a priest. He might be chosen from the second, or military caste; but he must become a priest before he could assume the sovereignty. It was a sufficient reason for this that the king must have always been an instructed person, and in fellowship with the class who held all the dignities and privileges of knowledge and of the sacred office. The sovereign in Egypt was assisted in his government by a council of priests; and of course it was necessary for him to hold, in common with his advisers, that knowledge and those secrets of custom by which the nation was governed. The rock in which the tombs of the kings were excavated is calcareous, full of veins and abounding in nuggets of flint.

Among the many tombs open to us, we may choose one for a brief examination; and the most attractive is that discovered by Belzoni, whose occupant was Osirei, father of Ramases the Great. We descended a flight of steps to a depth of 24 feet. To this stairway succeeds a passage of 18 1/2 feet by 9; passing another door, a second staircase descends in horizontal length 25 feet; beyond which two doorways and a passage of 29 feet bring you to a chamber 12 feet by 14, where a pit, filled up by Belzoni, once appeared to form the utmost limit of the tomb. Part of its inner wall was composed of blocks of hewn stone, closely cemented together, and covered with a smooth coat of stucco, like the other walls of this excavated catacomb, on which a continuation of those subjects that still adorn its remaining sides was depicted. In the first hall beyond the pit, about 26 feet square, there are four pillars that support the roof, which, as well as the walls, are decorated with highly-finished sculptures, which from their vivid colours appear but the work of yesterday. It is here that the first deviations from the general line of direction occur. Two passages and a chamber 17 feet by 14, communicating by a door with the grand hall 26 feet square and supported by six pillars are here displayed, the upper end terminating in a vaulted saloon 30 feet by 19, in whose centre stood an alabaster sarcophagus,—the cenotaph of the deceased monarch, upon the summit of an inclined plane, which, with a staircase on either side descends into the heart of the argillaceous rock for a distance of 150 feet. The total horizontal length of this catacomb is 320 feet, without the inclined descent below the sarcophagus, and its perpendicular depth 90 feet; but it measures in all a depth of about 180 feet. The walls are covered with painted sculptures and hieroglyphics beautifully drawn and written. The King is seen in the presence of the deities Athor, Horus, Anubis, Isis, Osiris, Nofri-Atmoo, and Pthah. Many other tombs of nearly equal size and importance remain in the valley,

9

but the foregoing may serve as an example of their general character (1).

Everyone must feel some interest in Egyptian works of art, for they have at least the great merit of originality; nor can any one deny the imposing grandeur of the Theban temples. Luxor, or Luksor, occupies part of the site of ancient Diospolis, and still holds the rank of a market town. A dromos, connecting the temple of Amunoph III. with Karnak, extended in front of two beautiful Obelisks of red granite, one of which still remains, the other is the one now in the place de la Concorde at Paris.

Behind the obelisks are two sitting statues of Ramases, one on each side of the pylon or gateway; but like the obelisk, they are much buried in the earth and sand which has accumulated around them. The principal entrance of the grand temple lies on the north-west side. Passing through the pylon, you arrive at a large open court 275 feet by 329, with a covered corridor on either side, and a double line of columns down the centre. The grand hall measures 170 feet by 329, sup-

(1) We visited some old excavations wherein a party of Arabs had taken up their abode, employing themselves in digging and searching for mummies: we saw eight of those which they had discovered, but not yet opened ; the people asked a price of from five to ten pounds for each.

We visited the tombs of the Queens, but did so with some difficulty, as the entrances are nearly choked up by sand falling down from the rocks above. But, inside, the passages and chambers, the ceilings and doorways, are all excavated regularly straight, and square at the angles. The surfaces have been covered with a white cement, laid on the walls about a quarter of an inch in thickness, that is now as hard as marble, and on this surface the hieroglyphics were written with a jet-black ink, and the figures drawn and coloured, all looking as fresh as if only done a few years ago.

ported by a central avenue of twelve massive columns, 66 feet high and 12 in diameter.

January 19th.—I called on Mustapha Aga, the consular agent at Luxor, and saw a collection of curiosities he had picked up at various times and places, with a number of mummies that were for sale.

January 21st. —It was with feelings of regret we now prepared to leave Thebes; and making our way down the Nile against a cold north wind, we anchored a few miles above Keneh.

January 22d.—The north wind continuing to blow bitterly cold, the poor men of our crew, being so lightly clothed, suffered intensely; the thermometer in our cabin with the windows shut, indicated only from 50 to 52° Fahr. at 2 p. m. The men, rowing all day against the wind, anchored in the evening at Keneh. We rode through the town, passing the bazaar, which is much larger than at most of the other towns. We visited a manufactory where those porous bottles that serve to cool the water used for drinking at Cairo and Alexandria are made. The mode of making those jars and bottles is very simple. The clay, which is found in the neighbourhood, is mixed with certain proportions of ashes obtained by burning the halfeh-grass. It is then ground by a wheel placed in a pit; when sufficiently ground it is laid on the turning table and formed into the bottles, which are dried in the sun and baked in an oven; they are then, without any glazing, ready for market.

January 23d.—We visited the temples at Dendera, which, though of gigantic proportions, cannot vie with those of Thebes. The principal one, dedicated to Isis, was erected under the Ptolemies nearly two thousand years ago. It has a grand portico, and the whole temple having a few years since been cleared of the sand with which it was filled , its proportions are clearly displayed; the walls and columns showed numerous figures and writings in a somewhat inferior style of art. We returned to the boat and passed down the river, having now seen the last of the grand temples, there being no other between this place and Cairo.

January 24th.—At a place called Howe, on the eastern bank, we landed for the purpose of seeing a Marabout, or Arab saint, who it is said took up his station on the naked sand, a little way up from the river, at this place some twenty-five years ago, and has remained there without a particle of clothing, or shelter of any kind to protect him against wind or sun. He is supplied with the few things necessary to keep him alive by the boatmen passing up or down the river ; none venture to pass by without contributing towards his support, and thus secure the benefit of his prayers in their behalf. His ability to live as he does, is a sufficient proof to them of his sanctity and of his miraculous preservation. He was a large muscular man about fifty years old, the hair of his head gray and matted in a filthy mass as large as a bushel. But he appeared in good health and condition.

We then passed down to Farshoot, where there is an extensive sugar factory.

January 25th.—The thermometer in our cabin stands at 50°. We started at 7 a.m. against a strong north wind, but made only six miles with hard rowing the whole day.

January 26th.—We reached Girgeh, the poor men worn out by cold and fatigue. Hassan having learned that some pirates were on the river between this place and Osioot, we decided upon remaining here till the next day.

January 27th.—A strong head wind is blowing, so we make but slow progress. We passed the body of a man floating down with the river; the face being downward we could only see that his skin was black and the head shaved, proving it to have been one of the natives. We went on to Soohag, and then to Gebel-Shekh Hereedee; the reis expressing much alarm and fear of the pirates, and praying anxiously for our safe arrival at Osioot.

January 30th.—We at length arrived at Osioot, and had I not experienced it, I could not have believed that in this latitude the temperature could have been so low as it has been for the past few days.

February 1st. — We arrived at Manfaloot and anchored for the night. The next morning was calm, so the men rowed cheerfully on till we came to a bend in the river, where they were able to use the sail for the first time since leaving Wadee Halfeh. We passed on to Beni Hassan, and anchored.

February 3d.—A cloudy morning, very unusual here. We crossed the river, and visited the excavations of Beni Hassan; the larger ones are like temples, having columns and architraves, as if they had been copied from constructed buildings; the paintings on the walls though very old are in good preservation.

February 4th. — The weather being calm, the men kept at their oars all night, but struck twice upon sandbanks from which they had much difficulty in getting off. The sky was cloudy this morning, and a little rain fell during the day, a rare occurrence here; but there is no rule without an exception. We stopped for the night, and put up an awning to keep the men dry.

February 5th. — The sky still cloudy, but the wind fair, so we passed on smoothly, by Beni Soeef, and anchored at the village of Eczawia.

February 6th. — Starting at 6 a.m. with a light south wind, we arrived at 6 p.m. at Bedresheyn, having seen this evening the tops of some pyramids, and anchored for the night.

February 7th. — We took donkeys this morning and visited the excavations lately discovered by a Frenchman, who was searching for antiquities under some mounds near the ancient Acropolis of Memphis, in the vicinity of Sakkara. In the excavation, there is a central gallery or hall 12 feet wide, about 500 yards long and 12 feet high, cut in the limestone rock, the ceiling of which is semicircular. On either side of this central passage are excavated twelve side-chambers, each about 14 feet wide, 12 feet high, and 30 feet deep, with semicircular ceilings cut in the rock, and solid masses of about 15 feet thick left standing as divisions between the chambers. In each chamber stands a huge sarcophagus of blue granite, 12 feet long, 7 wide, and 8 feet deep cut from a solid block, made perfectly square and polished on the surface, covered by a solid lid 4 feet thick; the insides cut out so as to be 5 feet wide in the clear, and the outsides of some of them covered with hieroglyphic writings, engraved on the granite. They had all been found open when discovered, the lids being slid off about a foot towards one end. Some of them contained skeletons of oxen, which showed they were made to contain the bodies of the sacred bulls Apis.

The greatest wonder with me, apart from the enormous labour required to prepare each of these monster sarcophagi, was how they had been introduced to their present positions. The ceilings are all of the solid rock, and the width of the central passage is not sufficient to allow the sarcophagi to be turned into the chambers, even if they had been lowered down by an opening from the surface into one end of the main passage. All is mystery in the works left by those ancient Egyptians.

From hence to Sakkara was a ride of about two miles across the desert; we there found ourselves among the remains of the Necropolis. It was a mournful confusion of whitened skulls, deep pits, mummy rags, and mounds of sand.

It was here that Herodotus rose into enthusiasm about the grandeur and wisdom of Egypt, and learned most of what he knew of its history. It was here that, in a later day, Abdallatif, the learned physician of Bagdad, complained of the mischief wrought by treasure seekers, who were even then separating the stones of the ancient buildings for the sake of the copper clamps which were used in joining them together. He says—" I am now speaking of the ruins of the old capital of this country, which was situated in the territory of Geezeh, a little above Fostat. This capital was Memphis : it was there that the Pharaohs resided ; and this city was the seat of empire in Egypt. It is of this city that we are to understand the words of God in the Koran, when he is speaking of Moses : *He entered into the city at the moment when the inhabitants were sinking into sleep.*

" For Moses made his abode in a village of the territory of Geezeh, a little way from the capital; which village was called Dimouh. The Jews have a synagogue there at this day. The ruins of Memphis now occupy a space which is half a day's journey every way. This city was flourishing in the time of Abraham, Joseph and Moses, and a long time before them, and a long time after them. "—" A man of good sense, seeing all these remains of antiquity, feels disposed to excuse that error of the vulgar which supposes that men of distant ages lived much longer than those of our times, or that they were of gigantic stature. We remain indeed in a sort of stupor when we consider how much of genius, of resolution and of patience, must have been united with a profound knowledge of geometry, to execute such works; what different instruments from any that we know of must have been employed; and what obstinate labour, and to what point these men have studied the structure of animals and of men." These are some few particulars of what Abdallatif saw among these ruins of Memphis seven centuries ago.

We next went to the mummy pits. Here were underground chambers, pillared, painted and sculptured, excavated into ornamented recesses, and consecrated to the gods, and destined for the burial of birds. In a sort of quarry lay strata of the bodies of cats, the rags fluttering out; the feline population of a whole continent for ages would be required, one would think, to fill these pits. The cats are swathed like the human body; the ibises are inclosed in red pots, like chimney-pots, with the round end cemented on.

There was nothing to be now seen about this buried city but a tomb or two — a sarcophagus here, or a mummy-case there. On our return to the river we saw a great number of men at work upon the causeway which crosses the plain: a large portion of their work consisted in carrying earth in frail baskets, which earth they scooped out with their hands without shovels or any other instruments. Such is the present state of manners and of art on the spot where Herodutus held counsel with the wise men of the world, and where the greatest works of man's hands were reared by means of science and art of which the world is now hardly capable.

Visit to the Pyramids.

February 10th.—On arriving at the elevated position where the pyramids of Geezeh stand, I was in some degree disappointed : instead of growing larger, they appeared to become less as we approached, until at last they came fully up to our preconception, except in being rougher on the surface and of a brighter tint. The platform on which the largest pyramid stands is higher than I had supposed; the Second pyramid, which at a distance looks as large as the other, here sinks surprisingly; this was to me the strongest evidence of the magnitude of the Great pyramid. To ascend the Great pyramid I set out with two Arab guides from the N.E. corner; on looking up it is not the magnitude of the ascent which makes one think it scarcely possible to achieve it, but the unrelieved succession of bright yellow steps, that stretch out in a long perspective to the top. The steps are each about four feet high, and the most difficult to ascend are the first six courses, which are broken and precipitous. From the platform on the summit, a splendid view is obtained of the surrounding country in all directions. On the S. W. corner, not far from the large pyramid stands the Second pyramid in its sunken area, surrounded by walls, and showing by the external casing, that is still left upon the upper part of it, how much finer these pyramids must have looked before they were dismantled of their casing. The descent as

far as the entrance to the interior may be accomplished
in ten minutes. From the entrance a passage runs up
a steep inclined plane with notches cut in the stone for
the feet, so as to prevent sliding down too rapidly;
unless at one place, the entrance upon the passage to
the King's chamber. The whole interior structure,
where visible, even the ceiling over the King's
chamber, is made of blocks of dark granite, joined
so closely that the edge of a penknife could scarcely
be anywhere inserted between them. There is
nothing now like it in the world, nor surely will there
ever be. The smoothness and finish of the surfaces so
deepen the gloom, that a feeling of horror and awe
creeps over one while gazing at the unrelieved surface.
Notwithstanding the clear view we obtained in the
chamber of the enormous blocks that form the ceiling
and the sides, the impression was less tremendous than
in the descending passage. There is nothing in the
chamber except the sarcophagus near one end, which is
sadly broken, but still rings like a bell when struck on
the side. The prodigious portcullises of granite in the
passage were more visible to us in going down than
when ascending, and how they were placed there was
in itself an oppressive speculation. We then ascended
to the Queen's chamber, along a passage above that to
the King's. This passage was not so low as we had
expected. The chief interest about the Queen's chamber
is from its being placed under the apex of the pyramid;
its ceiling is on this account pointed by the blocks composing it being set to stand against each other at the top,
like those forming the great entrance. It must be remembered that this structure, with its wonderful art and
bewildering grandeur was the work of men of five
thousand years ago, and is the oldest monument known

to exist in the world. If this is to us the beginning of the Arts —this which manifests the existence of so many appliances of art unknown to us now— how are we to speculate on what went before? And how completely do we find ourselves thrown out in all our notions of the duration of the human race!

There are five small rough chambers above the Queen's, evidently put there to lessen the superincumbent weight. There is a niche rather elaborately wrought. A pit has been opened below this niche, and Sir G. Wilkinson wishes that, if further search is made for the King's body, it should be by looking *under* this niche. It would be very desirable to have the pyramid more carefully explored down to the lowest point where any traces of works could be found. Works carried down so low must have had some purpose; and it might be well worth while to discover what that was. It is not satisfactory to suppose that subterranean structures were made merely to let the workmen out, after they had closed the upper passage by a granite portcullis. The great difficulty in exploring the pyramid is from the wonderful way in which the ancient builders closed these passages; the huge granite portcullises, blocking up the way, are almost insuperable. It is hard to distinguish them from the surrounding blocks, and to guess whether there may be a passage behind. I have a strong impression myself that, after all the wonders which have been laid open, there is still much to be discovered. If it be true that some one fired a pistol within the pyramid, and that the echoes were countless, that would seem to indicate that the edifice may be honeycombed with chambers. It becomes us, however, to be grateful for what we have learned. Colonel H. Vyse has laid the world under great obliga-

tions by his laborious exertions. He made among many
discoveries one of inestimable importance. He found
inscribed in the pyramid, in the most antique style,
the names of the Pharaohs who erected these edifices,
and they turn out to be the same given by Herodotus
and Manetho. It is now ascertained, beyond all
doubt, that these pyramids are the work of the Pharaohs
of the fourth dynasty; that is, of kings early
succeeding Menes, and living near the beginning of
the first period of Egyptian history. I suppose everyone knows the account given by Herodotus of the
building of this pyramid : how Cheops closed the temples, stopped the sacrifices, and made everybody work
for him at the buildings ;—how some quarried the stone
in the Arabian hills, and others conveyed it to the river
and over a bridge of boats ; while others drew it to the
spot where it was wanted ; and how it could be carried
across the plain only upon a causeway, which of itself took ten years to construct, and was a fine
work made of polished stones, with figures of animals
engraved thereon. How 100,000 men were employed
at a time, and were relieved by the same number at the
end of every three months ; how, much besides the ten
years occupied by the causeway, was required for
levelling the rock on which the edifice stands, besides
the twenty years for the building of the pyramid itself ;
how a machine, made of short pieces of wood, was
placed upon every step or course as the work proceeded,
for the purpose of raising the stones from step to step
as the work went on ; and how the filling up of these
gradations, to form the last smooth surface, was begun
from the top. How this surface bore engraved, for
Herodotus himself saw it, an inscription which told the
expense of the vegetables eaten by the labourers during

the progress of the work ; and how confounded the traveller declares himself to be, judging from the sum
spent in vegetables, at the thought of the expenditure
further necessary for the rest of the food, clothes of
the workmen and their iron tools, during the long
course of years required for the whole series of works
—among which he includes the subterranean structures,
which he again mentions as made by the King for
the purposes of sepulture, in an island formed by the
waters of the Nile, which he introduced into them by a
canal.

All this narrative is known to everybody who cares about
Egypt; and everybody has no doubt been struck by
this testimony to the use of iron tools and the existence
of polished stones, machinery, writing, and engraving,
between five and six thousand years ago. But everybody may not know what evidence we have of the solidity and the vastness of these works, in the impossibi-
lity which has been found of taking them to pieces.
This evidence is given by Abdallatif, whose book is so
little known that some passages relating to his visits
to the pyramids in or about A. D. 1190, translated by
De Sacy (Paris, 1810), have been found of great service.
He says— "The form which has been adopted in the
construction of the pyramids, and the solidity which has
been given to them, are well worthy of admiration. It
is to their form that they owe the advantage of having
resisted the hostility of centuries, or rather it seems as
if it were time which has resisted the opposition of
these eternal edifices.

"Indeed, when we meditate deeply on the construction
of the pyramids, we are compelled to acknowledge that
men of the greatest genius have here employed in combination their best powers, and that the subtlest minds

have exhausted their deepest resources ; that the most enlightened souls have exercised in profusion all the abilities that they possessed which could be applied to these constructions ; and that the wisest theory of geometry has employed all its means to produce these wonders as the last point of astonishment which it was possible to reach. Thus we may say that these edifices speak to us now of those who reared them, teach us their history, open to us in an intelligible manner the progress which they had made in the sciences and the excellence of their abilities : in a word, they put us in possession of the life and actions of the men of those days." After telling how the Pyramids are placed with regard to the points of the compass, and how this breaks the force of the wind, and what the gross measurements are, he goes on : — "Their pyramidal figure is truncated ; and the summit offers thereby a level of ten cubits every way. Here is a thing which I myself observed : when I visited them, there was in our party an archer, who let fly an arrow in the direction of the perpendicular height of one these pyramids, and in that of its thickness (its base); and the arrow fell a little short of midway. We learned that in the neighbouring village there were people accustomed to mount the pyramid, who did it without any difficulty. We sent for one of these men, and for a trifle which we gave him he set off up the pyramid, as we should to mount a staircase, and even quicker, without putting off either his shoes or his garments, which were very ample. I had desired him to measure, with his turban, the area at the top when he got there. When he came down, we took the measure of his turban, as it answered to that of the area at the summit. We found it to be eleven cubits, by the measure of the original cubit." — " One of these two pyramids is open, and offers an entrance by which the interior may be visited. This opening leads to narrow passages, to conduits which go down to a great depth, and to wells and precipices, as we are assured by such persons as have courage to explore them : for there are many people who are tempted by a foolish avarice and chimerical hopes into the interior of this edifice. They plunge into deep recesses, and come at last to a place where they find it impossible to penetrate further. As for the most frequented and ordinarily-used passage, it is a glacis which leads to the upper part of the pyramid, where there is a square chamber, and in this chamber a sarcophagus of stone. ''

Up to a recent date, there have been doubts whether the pyramid was open so long ago as this, and whether therefore the tradition was true which declares that Caliph Mamoon opened it, somewhere about A. D. 820. It is clear that in Abdallatif's time there was no novelty in its standing open ; and there seems no reason to doubt the narrative given by Arab writers of the opening by Caliph Mamoon. One of them, Abdel Hôkm, declares that a statue resembling a man (a mummy-case, no doubt) was found in the sarcophagus ; and within the statue, a human body, with a breastplate of gold and jewels, bearing written characters which no one understood.

Abdallatif says—''The opening by which the interior of the pyramid is reached at this day is not the original entrance ; it is a hole begun at random, and made by force. It is said it was Caliph Mamoon who made it. The greater part of our company entered it, and went up to the higher chamber. When they came down, they gave marvellous accounts of what they had seen ; and they said this passage was so full of bats and their dirt that it was almost stopped up: that the bats were nearly as large as pigeons; and that there were to be seen in the upper part open spaces and windows, which seemed to be intended to admit air and light. In another visit which I made to the pyramids, I entered this interior passage with several persons, and went about two-thirds of the way along it; but having become insensible through fear which struck me in this ascent, I came down again half dead. These pyramids are constructed of great stones from ten to twenty cubits long, and two or three cubits in breadth and thickness. The most admirable particular of the whole is the extreme nicety with which these stones have been prepared and adjusted. Their adjustment is so precise that not even a needle or a hair can be inserted between any two of them. They are joined by a cement laid on to the thickness of a sheet of paper. I cannot tell what this mortar is made of, it being of a substance entirely unknown to me.

"*These stones are covered with writing in that unknown character whose import is at this day wholly unknown.* I have not met in Egypt with any person who could say that he knew, even by hearsay, of any one who understood this character. *These inscriptions are so multitudinous, that if those only which are seen on the surface of these two pyramids were copied upon paper, more than ten thousand pages would be filled with them.*"

When we remember that Abdallatif is telling us what he himself saw, we cannot but admit this particular of his simple narrative. He goes on — " I have read in some books of the ancient Sabeans, that, of these two pyramids, one is the tomb of Agathodemon, and the other that of Hermes. These are, they say, two great prophets; but Agathodemon is the older and greater of the two. They say that from all countries of the world, people come in pilgrimage to these two pyramids.—In my great work, I have enlarged upon this subject; and I have related what others have said of these edifices. To that account, I refer those who desire further details. Here, I limit myself to what I have myself seen.

" When Melic-Alaziz Othman-ben-Yousouf had succeeded his father, he let himself be persuaded by some of his courtiers—foolish people—to demolish these pyramids : and they began with the red pyramid, which is the third and smallest of the three great pyramids.

"The Sultan sent there his sappers, miners and quarrymen, under the superintendence of some of the principal officers and first Emirs of his court, and gave them orders to destroy it. To execute these orders, they established their camp near the pyramid: they collected there a multitude of labourers from all quarters, and maintained them at great cost. They remained there eight entire months, occupied, with all their people, in executing their commission, carrying away, each day, after extreme exertion and exhaustion, two or three stones.

" Some pushed them from above with wedges and levers, while others drew them away from the base with ropes and cables. Whenever one of these stones fell, it made a fearful noise, which echoed far off, shook the earth, and made the hills tremble. By its fall, it was buried in the sand ; and then great efforts were made to remove it : after which, the people wrought grooves for the wedges to enter, and thus the stones were split into several pieces :—then each fragment was placed upon a car, to be carried to a mountain a little way off, and thrown out at its foot.

10

" After the company had remained a long time en-
camped on this spot, when their pecuniary means were
all expended, while their trouble and fatigue went on
increasing, and their resolution growing weaker, day by
day, and their strength was utterly exhausted, they
were obliged ignominiously to quit their enterprise.

" Far from obtaining the result they had anticipated,
and succeeding in their design, they ended by doing
nothing but spoiling the pyramid, and evidencing their
own powerlessness.

"This passed in the year A.D. 1196. When one now
looks at the stones brought down in the course of the
demolition, one is persuaded that the pyramid has been
destroyed from its foundation : but when, on the other
hand, one looks up at the pyramid, one believes that
it has suffered no injury whatever, and that nothing has
happened but the paring off of a portion of the casing on
one of its sides.

" Observing one day what extremely heavy work it
was to remove a single stone, I addressed one of the
superintendents who was directing the workmen, and
put this question to him — 'If any one offered you a thousand pieces of gold to replace one of these stones, and
adjust it as it was before, do you think you could accomplish it?' His answer was that if many times as much
was offered, they could not do such a thing ; and this he
affirmed with an oath. " (*Relation de l'Egypt*, livre I,
chap. 4.)

I fear that all such descriptions are thrown away, in
regard to the object of giving to the readers of them
any idea of what the pyramids are. They are useful
as records, however, and extremely interesting to travellers in going over the ground.

Dimensions of the Great pyramid, as measured by Colonel Vyse, in English feet :

Original base before the casing was removed :

    Length of side. . . . . . . 764 » feet.
    Perpendicular height. . . . 480,3/4 —

Present base since the casing was removed :

    Length of side. . . . . . . 746 » feet.
    Perpendicular height. . . . 450,3/4 —

	Acres.	Roods.	Poles.
Former area of base.	13	1	22
Present area of base.	12	3	3

The solid contents of the pyramid have been calculated at 85,000,000 cubic feet. And that there is space enough in this mass of masonry for 3,700 rooms of the same size as the King's chamber, leaving the contents of every second chamber solid by way of separation.

Of the Sphinx, Sir G. Wilkinson tells us : " Pliny says it measured from the belly to the highest part of the head sixty three feet: its length was one hundred and fort -three : and the circumference of its head round the forehead one hundred and two feet; all cut out of the natural rock, and worked smooth. " The ridge of the back, and the neck and head are all that can now be seen of it, the rest of the figure is covered up by the sands of the desert which have accumulated around it. What do we not owe to the ancient Egyptians, to their turn for engraving and painting ! Here is a people living only in the ideas they have bequeathed to us, and in the undecayed works of their hands!

No one of that great race survives : we have their corpses in abundance, but we do not know what their complexion was : their language is lost, except as studious men pick it up, word by word, with painful uncertainty, from an obscure cypher.

They teach us to be modest and patient in regard to our knowledge of the ancient world, by showing us that while we have been talking confidently of the six thousand years of human existence, we have in reality known nothing about it.   They rebuke us sufficiently in showing us that at that time men were living and acting very much as we do now—without some knowledge that we have gained, but in possession of some arts which we have not.   They confound us by the pictured exhibitions of their iron tools and steel armour; their great range of manufactures, and their feasts and sports so like our own.   In their kitchens, they decant wine by a syphon, and strew their sweet cakes with seeds, and pound their spices in a mortar.   In the drawing-room, they lounge on *chaises-longues*, and the ladies knit and net as ladies now do.   Doctor Abbott, at Cairo, had in his possession a piece of mending left unfinished several thousand years ago, which any woman of the present day might be proud of.   In the country we see the agriculturists taking stock ; and in the towns, the population divided into castes, subject to laws, and living under a theocracy, long before the generally believed time of the deluge.   There is enough here to teach us some humility and patience about the true history of the world.

All knowledge is sacred.   All truth is divine.   We may not like to be perplexed by new knowledge which throws us out of some notions which we took for knowledge before.   We are apt to feel our own privileges lessened by learning that knowledge existed for many ages before the time which we had supposed ; but I would ask whether the great guiding ideas of mankind are the more or the less venerable for having existed for some thousands of years longer than we had imagined ; and whether it is or is not a testimony to the power of those ideas that they raised into spiritual light a race which thereby became the greatest in the ancient world, preserved their empire through a longer duration than that of any other known people, and were made the source of enlightenment to nations then and still unborn?

The immense size of many of the coverings of apertures, and whole roofs of temples formed of one entire stone, still extant in Egypt, would stagger belief, if the truth were not so well authenticated. One fact is hereby proved—that the principles of the arch were then unknown, or the roof of the temple of Latona at Butis would not have been transported from the island of Philæ, as Herodotus testifies, a distance of nearly two hundred league. This roof was sixty feet square and four feet thick—the most enormous block of stone ever moved by human power, containing fourteen thousand four hundred cubic feet of granite. All modern mechanical powers must vanish before these wonderful exploits of ancient skill. Those of recent date which have been most extolled are as nothing in comparison. The moving and raising the Obelisk in front of St. Peter's at Rome, or that in the Place de la Concorde at Paris, only equal their first erection in Egypt, and fall infinitely short of the power required to separate them from their original bed in the quarry. Yet what wonder and amazement did these works of Pope Sextus and of Louis-Philippe excite at the time! Delineations of the machinery, and of the manner of applying it, were thought worthy of publication, and certainly do honour to the memory of the engineers and of their illustrious employers.

On the 17th of February we quitted the boat which had been our home for the last three months with feelings of regret, and removed to Sheppard's Hotel at Cairo. After a few days passed pleasantly there, we began to make preparations for a journey across the desert to Jerusalem; but erysipelas attacking my head, I was confined to my room for a month, and was thus rendered incapable of undertaking the journey, so we had to content ourselves with resolving to attempt it on some future occasion.

On the 18th of March we left Cairo for Alexandria, whence we went by the Austrian steamer to Corfu, where we remained for a month; and then by way of Messina, Naples, and Marseilles, we arrived at Paris, that pride of the world and centre of civilization.

ERRATA.

Page 3, line 15, read five..... ... instead of six.

— 16 — 27, — round......   —   rung.

— 24 — 7, — storey......   —   store.

— 24 — 20, — afterwards..   —   afterwads.

— 33 — 16, — and thus accomplish. instead of by thus accomplishing.

Paris.—Printed by E Brière, rue Saint-Honoré, 257.

ILLUSTRATIONS

Unless otherwise indicated, all buildings
illustrated in this section
are or were located in New Orleans.

1. James Gallier's business card, *c.*1833.
Tulane University Library, Labrot Collection.

POPULAR LECTURES

ON

ARCHITECTURE,

BY

J. GALLIER, ARCHITECT.

The first of a Course of Seven Lectures on Architecture, will be given in the Large Room of the Classical Hall, Washington Street, Brooklyn, on Tuesday Evening, the 25th of February, to commence at half-past seven o'clock, and to be continued on the evenings of every Friday and Tuesday, until the Course is completed.

Synopsis of the Course.

FIRST LECTURE.

Origin and Character of Architecture. Antediluvian Remains. Architecture considered as an Art; its Types and Prefigurations. Historical Sketch of the Art among the Assyrians, Chaldeans, Egyptians, Phœnicians, and ancient Jews. More particularly considered in Egypt, with illustrative Drawings and Examples of its style and modes of construction. The Art investigated among the nations of India, the ancient Hindûs, and other Eastern people. Excavations in Salsette, Ellora, and Elephanta: their use and origin considered.

SECOND LECTURE.

Persepolitan, Phœnician, Hebraic, and Chinese Architecture,with their characteristics. Architecture of the ancient Mexicans: their Pyramids, Temples, and Military Fortifications described and compared with those of Egypt and India.

THIRD LECTURE.

Architecture of the Greeks. The constituent elements of their earliest style defined. Investigation of the means by which it was brought to perfection. Their Temples, with the original types from which they drew their proportions. The Greek Orders. Characteristics of the Doric, as exhibited in the Parthenon.

FOURTH LECTURE.

The founding of Athens, Thebes, and other Cities of Ancient Greece, down to the age of Pericles. The Orders and their Divisions illustrated: their application and modes of construction. The Seven Orders of Temples. The Architecture of Greece traced through its Colonies, till its establishment in Etruria. Character of the Etruscan School.

FIFTH LECTURE.

The Etruscan School continued, till the conquest of Greece by the Romans. Roman Architecture, from the conquest of Greece to the time of Augustus. The Roman system of Orders illustrated: their Buildings, Temples, and methods of construction. The History of the Art carried on to Hadrian, and from thence till its immersion in the dark ages.

SIXTH LECTURE.

The Origin of Architecture in Britain, France, &c. Druidical Remains in England, Ireland, Scotland, France, and America · the Cromlechs, Excavations, Round Towers of Ireland, &c. with conjectures thereon. Gothic Architecture illustrated and traced to its elementary principles. Revival of Classic Architecture in Italy: its progress in Modern Europe.

SEVENTH LECTURE.

Examination of the most celebrated Buildings of Modern Europe and America. Investigation of the most appropriate styles for Public and Private Edifices in this country. Examination of the propriety of erecting Domes and Towers in Public Buildings. Architecture in America; its future prospects, and the means required to bring it to perfection.

☞ *Admission for the Course One Dollar, and for a Single Lecture 25 Cents.*

Tickets to be had of Mr. W. BIGLOW, Bookseller, No. 55, Fulton-Street, Brooklyn, and at the Classical Hall.

3. "The Three Sisters" (center building), Rampart Street at Bienville, Gallier and Dakin, architects, 1834. Demolished *c.*1950. Gallery detail. Photograph by Richard Koch, *c.*1934.

4.   "The Three Sisters" (center building). Photograph by Richard Koch, *c.*1934.

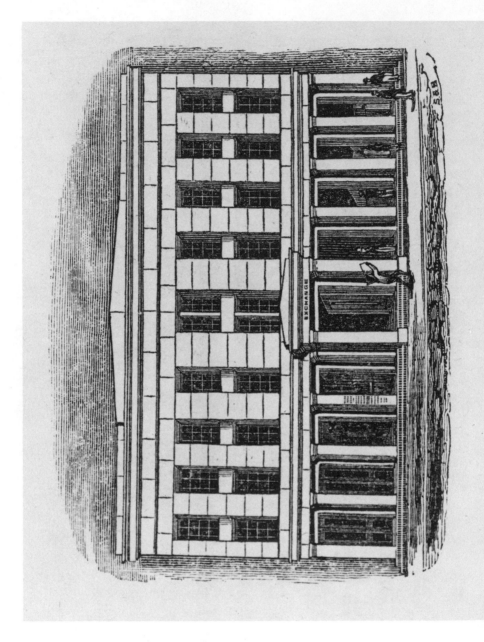

5. Merchants' Exchange, Gallier and Dakin, architects, 1835. Royal Street facade. From Norman's *New Orleans and Environs* (1845).

6. Merchants' Exchange. Exchange Place facade. Photograph by Samuel Wilson, Jr.

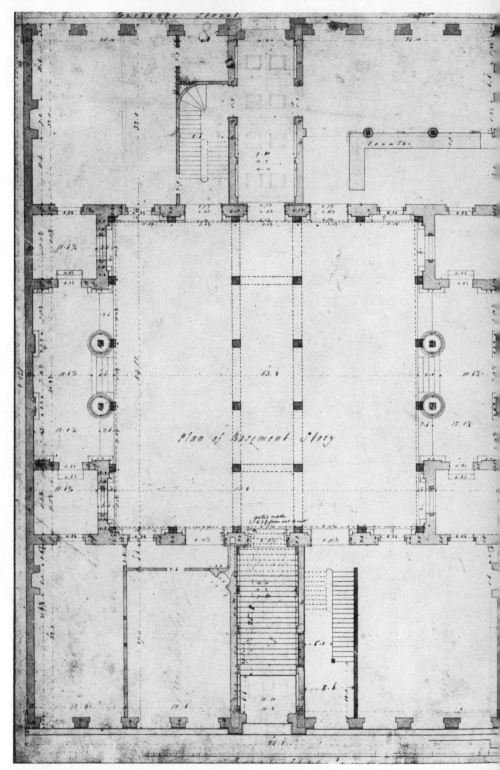

7. Merchants' Exchange. Floor plans, 1835, signed "Gallier & Dakin Arch[ts]" and showing Gallier's alterations for converting the Exchange to the Post Office in 1841.
L. V. Huber Collection.

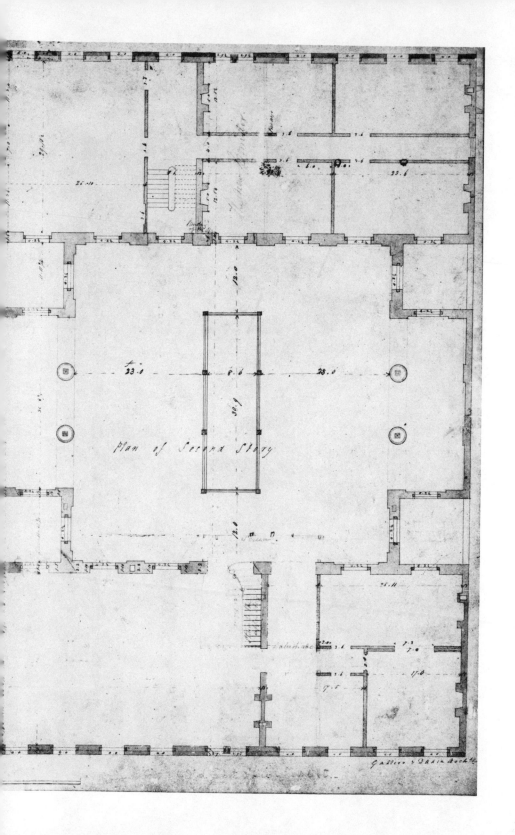

Plan of Second Story

Gallier & Dakin Arch^ts

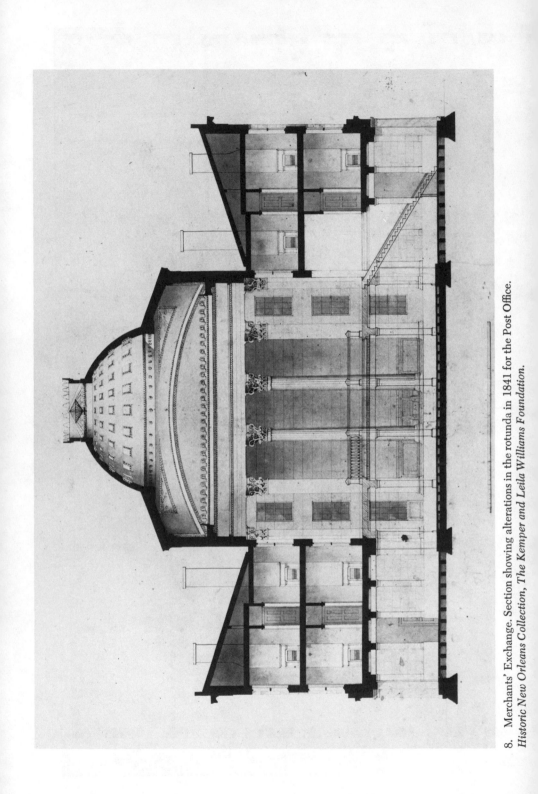

8. Merchants' Exchange. Section showing alterations in the rotunda in 1841 for the Post Office.
Historic New Orleans Collection, The Kemper and Leila Williams Foundation.

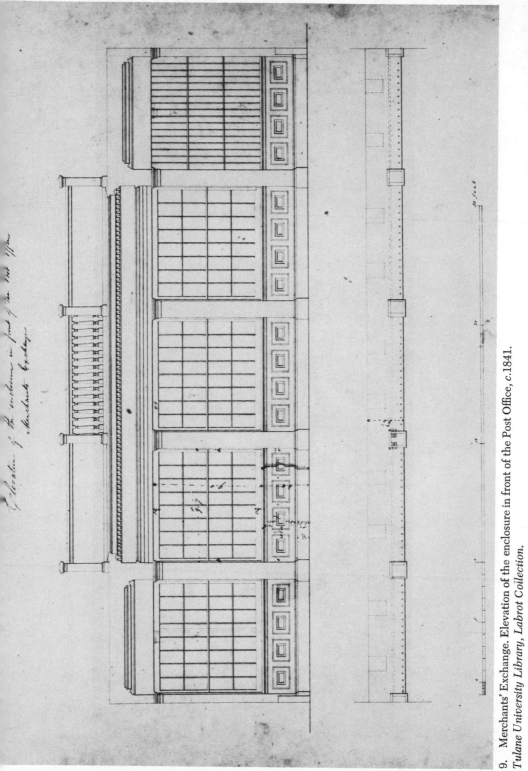

9. Merchants' Exchange. Elevation of the enclosure in front of the Post Office, c.1841.
Tulane University Library, Labrot Collection.

10.   Merchants' Exchange. Detail of rotunda cornice and pilaster. Photograph by Bernadas-Weis, 1959.

11. Christ Church, Canal Street at Bourbon, Gallier and Dakin, architects,
1835. The adjacent parsonage house erected 1825, Benjamin Fox, builder.
From a lithograph by J. Lion, 1846. *Richard Koch Collection.*

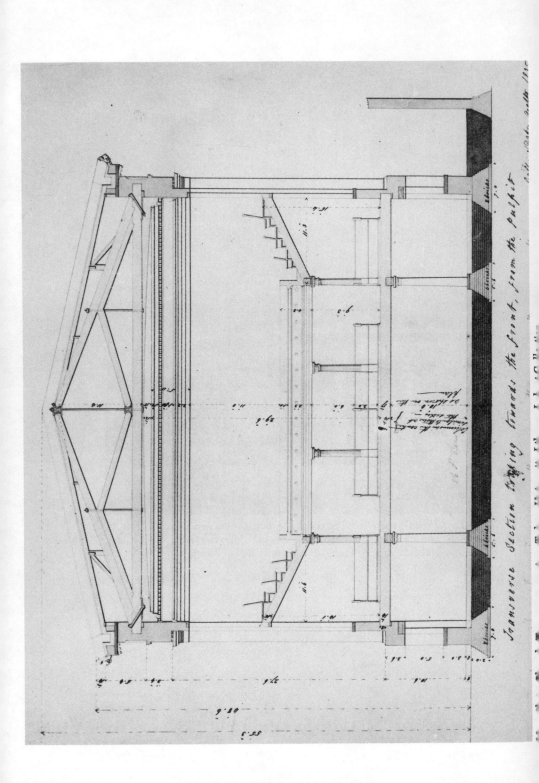

Transverse Section looking towards the Front, from the Pulpit

13. St. Charles Hotel, Gallier and Dakin, architects, 1835.
Lithograph by B.W. Thayer & Co., Boston, 1845. *Louisiana State Museum.*

14. St. Charles Hotel as restored without the dome after the fire of 1851.
Photograph by Mugnier, *c.*1885.

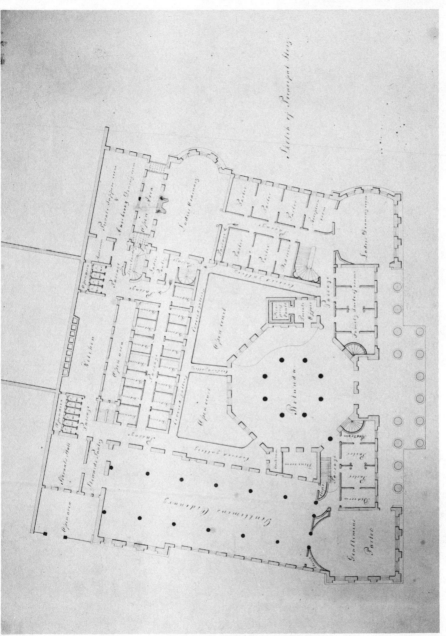

15.   St. Charles Hotel. Plan of first (street) floor.
Louisiana State Museum.

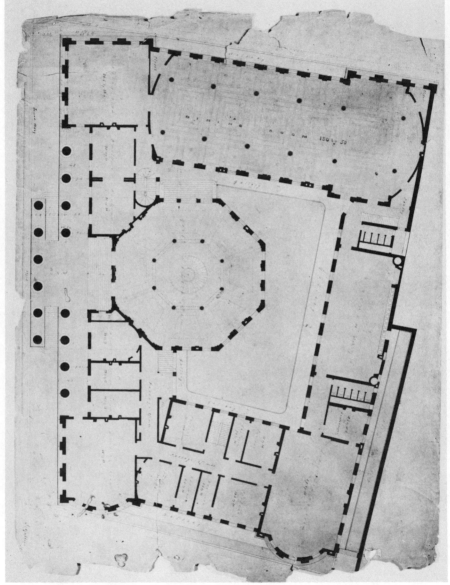

16.   St. Charles Hotel. Plan of second (main) floor.
Louisiana State Museum.

17.   Row of houses for Paloc and Dufour, Burgundy Street at Dumaine, James Gallier, architect and builder, 1838. Photograph by Samuel Wilson, Jr., 1950.

18.   St. Patrick's Church. High altar designed by James Gallier, 1839.
Mural paintings by Leon Pomarede, 1841. Photograph by Guy F. Bernard, 1958.

19. St. Patrick's Church. Wood, plaster, and stained glass vaulting of apse and side aisles designed by James Gallier, 1839. Photograph by Guy F. Bernard, 1958.

20. Ashland Plantation, Geismar, La., residence of Duncan F. Kenner, c.1841. Design attributed to James Gallier. Photograph by Richard Koch, c.1927.

21.   Residence for William Newton Mercer (now the Boston Club), 824 Canal Street, James Gallier, architect, 1844. Photograph by Richard Koch, 1945.

22.   Commercial Exchange (later the Masonic Temple), St. Charles Street at Perdido, James Gallier, architect-builder, 1845. Photograph by Mugnier, *c*.1885.

23.   Christ Church, Canal Street at Dauphine.
Thomas K. Wharton's first rough sketch of a design, 1845. *New York Public Library*.

24.   Christ Church as built by James Gallier, 1847. To the left is one of the wings of "Union Terrace," a group of four residences, Dakin and Dakin, architects, 1836–1837. Photograph by Mugnier, *c.*1885.

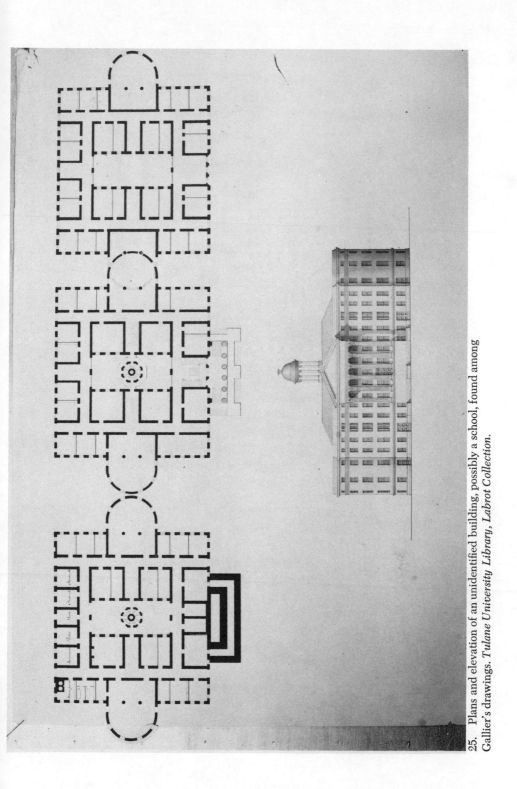

25. Plans and elevation of an unidentified building, possibly a school, found among Gallier's drawings. *Tulane University Library, Labrot Collection.*

MUNICIPAL HALL

LAFAYETTE SQUARE NEW ORLEANS.

26. Municipal Hall, Lafayette Square (formerly the old City Hall, now Gallier Hall), James Gallier, architect, 1845. Lithograph by F. Bedford, London, from a drawing by Thomas K. Wharton. *Historic New Orleans Collection, The Kemper and Leila Williams Foundation.*

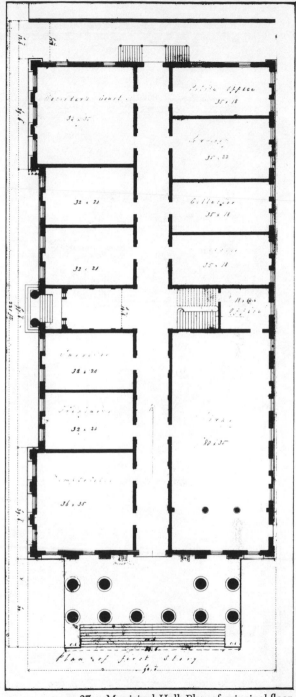

27. Municipal Hall. Plan of principal floor.
Tulane University Library, Labrot Collection.

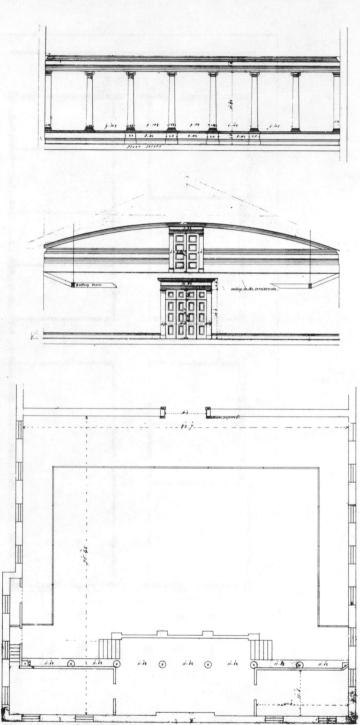

28. Municipal Hall. Plan and elevations of the Lyceum Hall, second floor.
Tulane University Library, Labrot Collection.

29. Municipal Hall. Section and reflected ceiling plan of Lyceum Hall, approved March 14, 1844. *Tulane University Library, Labrot Collection.*

30. Municipal Hall. The pediment sculpture, representing Liberty supporting Justice and Commerce, is by Robert A. Launitz, 1850. Photograph by Mugnier, *c.*1885.

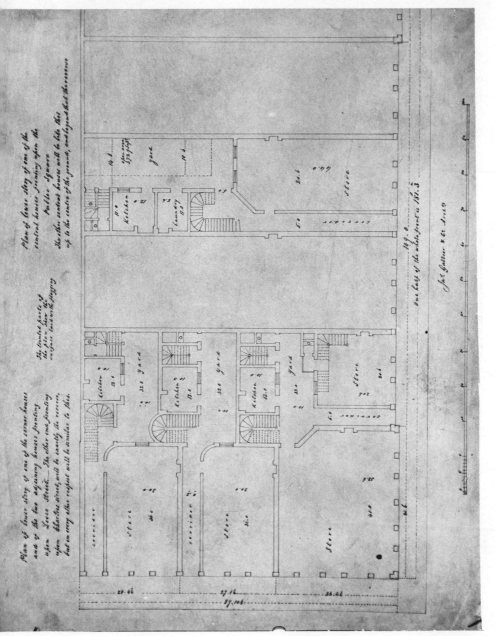

31. Pontalba Buildings, Jackson Square, 1849. Partial plan of first floor signed "Ja.ˢ Gallier & Co. Arch.ᵗˢ " *Upper Pontalba Commission.*

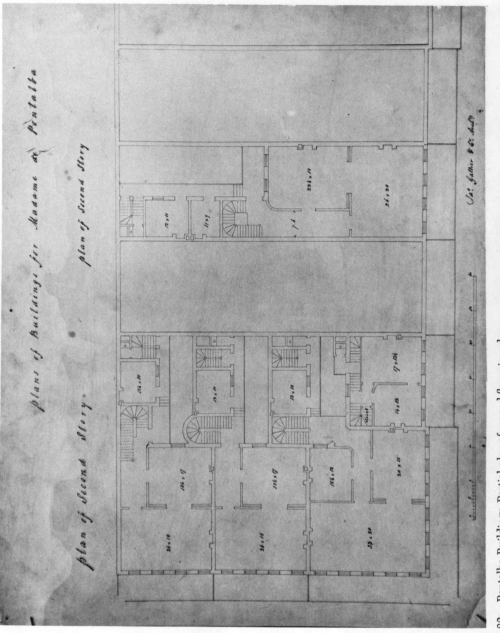

32. Pontalba Buildings. Partial plan of second floor signed

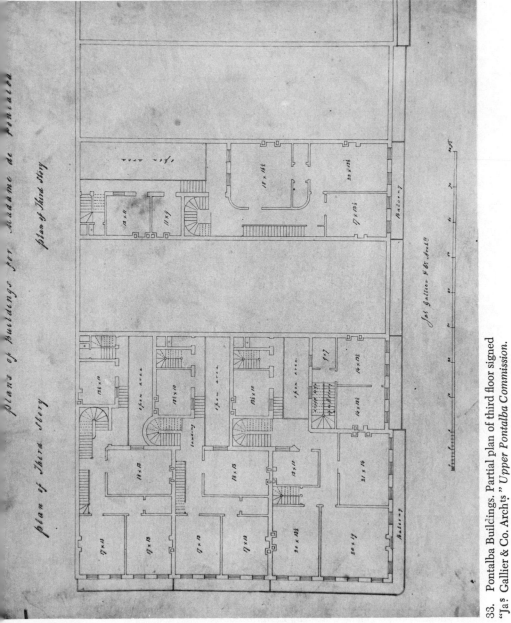

33. Pontalba Buildings. Partial plan of third floor signed
"Ja⁵ Gallier & Co. Arch⁵" *Upper Pontalba Commission.*

34.   Unidentified store. Elevation signed "Gallier, Turpin & Co. Arch ^{ts}"
and dated March 1, 1850. *Tulane University Library, Labrot Collection.*

35. General Seafoods, Inc., Tchoupitoulas Street. Design attributed to Gallier, Turpin & Co. Photograph by Richard Koch *c*.1937.

36.   Monument to James Gallier designed by James Gallier, Jr., 1866, St. Louis Cemetery No. 3, Esplanade Avenue. Photograph by Samuel Wilson, Jr., 1950.

37. Gallier House, 1132 Royal Street, James Gallier, Jr., architect and builder, 1857. *Gallier House.*

38. Courtyard in the rear of Gallier House. *Gallier House.*